CLIMATES BEFORE AND AFTER THE GENESIS FLOOD:

Numerical Models and their Implications

by

Larry Vardiman, Ph.D.

2001

First Printing 2001

Climates Before and After the Genesis Flood:
Numerial Models and their Implications

Copyright © 2001

Institute for Creation Research
P.O. Box 2667
El Cajon, California 92021

Cataloging in Publication Data
Library of Congress Catalog Card Number: 00 135926
ISBN 0-932766-63-3

ALL RIGHTS RESERVED

No portion of this book may be used in any form without written permission of the publishers, with the exception of brief excerpts in magazine articles, reviews, etc.

Printed in San Diego

ACKNOWLEDGEMENTS

This monograph is dedicated to my oldest daughter Michelle who with her husband Victor are raising my two grandchildren Spencer and Carter. Michelle almost always exhibits a friendly smile and a positive outlook. As a serious scientist type I don't tell her how much I love her as often as I should.

I thank Kenneth Cumming for his review of this monograph. As usual he always catches editorial mistakes that I have made, particularly missing references. Any errors still remaining, are, of course, mine.

This is primarily a summary document and much of the material was published in prior ICR monographs and articles published by the Creation Research Society Quarterly, the Creation Ex Nihilo Technical Journal, and the International Conferences on Creationism. Some of the text was taken from theses and articles written by my students David Rush, Karen (Spelman) Bousselot, Jim Zavacky, and Nancy Zavacky. Herman Daily revised much of the Fortran code for CCM1 and was responsible for getting LINUX and VIS5D to run on our PCs. Data for the ice cores and sea floor sediment were provided by the National Geophysical Data Center in Boulder, Colorado. Original computer codes for CCM1, MM5, and VIS5D were provided by the National Center for Atmospheric Research in Boulder, Colorado. The starting data for simulation of Hurricane Florence were provided by George Lai at NASA Goddard in Baltimore, Maryland. Other hurricane animations and images were also provided by NASA Goddard. The numerical processing for this research was conducted on computer equipment provided by Steve Low and his associates with the Hewlett-Packard Company and Phil Barksdale. Jim and Penny Moyers, the Mobil Oil Corporation, and many others also donated funds to this work.

I thank ICR for providing the opportunity and facilities to conduct the research supporting this monograph and for publishing my findings. I continue to enjoy ". . . thinking God's thoughts after Him . . ."

TABLE OF CONTENTS

CHAPTER	SUBJECT	PAGE
1	Introduction	1
2	A Vapor Canopy Model	7
	Distribution of Water Vapor with Height	8
	Diffusion of Water Vapor Downward	12
	Radiational Properties of a Vapor Canopy	16
	Sensitivity Studies of a Vapor Canopy Model	19
3	Helium Escape from the Atmosphere	23
	Introduction	23
	Thermal Escape of Helium	23
	Non-thermal Escape of Helium	38
	Conclusions and Recommendations	39
4	Ice Core Analyses	41
	A Young-Earth Age Model for Ice Cores	42
	The Conventional Explanation for the Variation in Oxygen Isotopes in Ice Cores	54
	Ice Core Data	55
	A Young-earth Explanation for the Variation in Oxygen Isotopes in Ice Cores	59
	Precipitation Trajectories	60
	Horizontal Dispersion of Oxygen Isotopes	65
	Application to Ice Shelves	67
	Conclusions and Recommendations	67
5	Sea-floor Sediment Accumulation	69
	Introduction	69
	A Young-earth Age Model	71
	Applications of a Young-earth Age Model	75
	Implications of a Young-earth Age Model	77

CHAPTER	SUBJECT	PAGE
6	Global Climate Modeling with CCM1	81
	Introduction	81
	The General Circulation of Today's Atmosphere	82
	Climate Modeling	84
	Description of the Community Climate Model	85
	Paleoclimates and Future Climates	86
	Uniformly Warm Oceans	86
	A Sensitivity Study of Warm Sea-Surface Temperature	87
	Simulation of Precipitation Induced by Hot Mid-Ocean Ridges	88
	Climate Model Limitations	92
7	Future Research with MM5	93
	Hurricane Modeling	93
	Other Mesoscale Modeling	99
	Dispersion of Oxygen Isotopes	99
	Changes in Flow Patterns and Precipitation over the Colorado River Basin	99
	Hurricane-Generated Hummocky Cross-bedding	100
8	Computer Hardware and Software Used at ICR	101
	References	103

LIST OF FIGURES

FIGURE	CAPTION	PAGE
2.1	Temperature as a function of altitude for a two-layer atmosphere	9
2.2	Pressure as a function of altitude in a two-layer vapor canopy model	11
2.3	Schematic of layers in canopy model	14
2.4	Rate of diffusion of water vapor downward with time	15
2.5	Vertical temperature distributions as a function of time	17
2.6	Equilibrium temperatures for various canopies	18
2.7	Equilibrium vertical temperature profiles as a function of solar constant	20
3.1	Escape speed *vs.* distance from the surface of the earth	31
3.2	Gaussian speed distribution function	33
3.3	Three-dimensional velocity space	33
3.4	Maxwellian speed distribution function	34
3.5	Geometry relating the upward vertical component of velocity	35
4.1	$\delta^{18}O$ *vs.* depth for Camp Century, Greenland	43
4.2	Flow model of ice flowing outward from an ice divide	44
4.3	Schematic of time and height variables of a layer of an ice sheet	45
4.4	Nye model age *vs.* height above base for Camp Century	46
4.5	$\delta^{18}O$ *vs.* the conventional time for Camp Century, Greenland	47
4.6	Thickness of the Camp Century ice sheet as a function of time	50
4.7	Position of ice layers at Camp Century as a function of time	52
4.8	$\delta^{18}O$ *vs.* young-earth time for Camp Century, Greenland	53
4.9	$\delta^{18}O$ *vs.* depth for Camp Century, Greenland	56
4.10	$\delta^{18}O$ *vs.* depth for Dye-3, Greenland	57
4.11	$\delta^{18}O$ *vs.* depth for Summit, Greenland	58
4.12	Initial position of 12 particles in a typical wind field	62
4.13	Trajectories of graupel in a 100 cm/sec maximum vertical wind	63
4.14	Trajectories of spatial crystals in a 100 cm/sec maximum vertical wind	64
4.15	Trajectories of dendritic crystals in a 100 cm/sec maximum vertical wind	64
4.16	Dispersion of $\delta^{18}O$ *vs.* distance from edge of ice shelf	66
5.1	$\delta^{18}O$ in sea-floor sediments *vs.* depth for site V28-238	70
5.2	Age of a sediment layer from the young-earth age model *vs.* height	73
5.3	$\delta^{18}O$ in sea-floor sediments *vs.* conventional time from DSDP sites	74
5.4	Paleotemperature derived from $\delta^{18}O$ in sea-floor sediment	75
5.5	Polar ocean bottom temperature *vs.* time after the Flood	77
5.6	Equatorial Pacific ocean surface temperature *vs.* time after the Flood	78
6.1	The general circulation of today's atmosphere	83
6.2	Precipitation contours from day 360 of the run with 30°C oceans	88
6.3	Grid points used in CCM1	89
6.4	Precipitation rate for grid points over a ridge of 70°C	89
6.5	Horizontal wind field at a pressure of 110 mb (15 km)	91
6.6	Horizontal wind field at a pressure of 500 mb (5 km)	91

FIGURE	**CAPTION**	**PAGE**
7.1	Hurricane Gladys in the Gulf of Mexico	97
7.2	Simulation of Hurricane Florence at 5 hrs.	98
7.3	Simulation of Hurricane Florence at 13 hrs.	98
7.4	Simulation of Hurricane Florence at 21 hrs.	99
7.5	Simulation of Hurricane Florence at 29 hrs.	99
7.6	Cold "footprint" produced by Hurricane Bonnie	100

LIST OF TABLES

TABLE	CAPTION	PAGE
2.1	Normal values and their ranges used in the sensitivity study	20
3.1	Composition of the atmosphere	24
4.1	List of parameters in the young-earth ice sheet flow model	54

CHAPTER 1

INTRODUCTION

On July 21, 1969 the *Eagle* landed on the Moon as part of the Apollo program. On the way to and from the Moon, Earth could be seen by man in its full splendor from God's vantage point for the first time. Neil Armstrong stated during one of his transmissions to mission control that, "Earth looks like a Christmas tree ornament hung in space." The blue ocean and sky, the white clouds and polar ice caps, and the brown continents all contrasted sharply with the absolute blackness of space punctuated by millions of stars. Of all the planets, Earth exhibits the most beautiful panorama of colors and shapes seen in our solar system. It is apparent that God designed man's home to be one of the most beautiful places in the universe.

The blue tinge of the light scattered and reflected through the atmosphere is a major contributor to the beauty of Earth as seen from space. God designed the size and characteristics of the oxygen and nitrogen molecules to interact with the white light from the Sun and produce a canopy of blue light during the daytime. The atmosphere appears as a pastel, transparent shell from space, but from the surface of the Earth it produces a spherical canopy of blue light which blots out the stars, permitting only the Sun and Moon to be seen during the day. At night the scattered light disappears, allowing us to see through the atmosphere to the stars.

This canopy of air is not only beautiful, but provides a cocoon of oxygen for man and all other air-breathing organisms. Without this sea of air held to the Earth by gravity we would quickly die in the vacuum of space. The atmosphere also moderates the temperature of the Earth's surface and transports water vapor as part of the hydrologic cycle. The weather and climate patterns on Earth are strongly dependent upon the interaction of the Sun's radiation with our atmosphere. The climate and weather, in turn, affect many biological and geophysical systems. It is interesting and useful to understand more about how our atmosphere operates.

It is apparent from the geological record that atmospheric conditions have not always been as we know them today. Distributions and magnitudes of temperature, precipitation, wind, and even chemical constituents of the atmosphere appear to have varied greatly in the past. Geophysicists and geologists conclude that oxygen concentrations were much less and carbon dioxide concentrations much greater. They suggest that temperatures have oscillated greatly during a series of dozens or maybe even hundreds of ice ages and interglacials. Precipitation rates and accumulations have been much greater in some locales during the ice ages and much less in others during the interglacials. Over longer periods of time variations in the shape, topography and location of the continents on the Earth have produced sedimentary deposits which suggest even more dramatic changes in oxygen, carbon dioxide, and water vapor distributions. These variations have occurred slowly over millions and even billions of years according to scientists who adopt the conventional, evolutionary time scales. During this long period plants and animals would have had time to evolve, producing a feedback effect on the atmosphere.

But, what if the evidence for all these paleoclimatic effects is not due to many low-energy events over millions or billions of years? What if the effects were due to a single, catastrophic event which occurred only a few thousand years ago? What if the Genesis Flood described in the Bible actually happened and the entire crust, ocean, and atmosphere were disrupted as violently as suggested in Scripture? Would this event and the ensuing aftermath be an adequate explanation for the changes in the Earth's atmosphere commonly attributed to long, slow changes?

The purpose of this monograph is to review the research accomplished in the area of paleoclimatology by Dr. Vardiman and his students at the Institute for Creation Research (ICR) and outline research plans for the future. The distinctive approach taken by Dr. Vardiman has been to analyze climate and weather data available through standard meteorological sources and adapt and exercise conventional climate models available from various government and university laboratories using catastrophic, young-earth conditions. Results of this research are then compared with descriptions and expectations from processes and events found in the Bible, particularly those associated with Creation and the Genesis Flood.

Biblical paleoclimatology has been the focus of a research program at the Institute for Creation Research for almost twenty years. When Dr. Larry Vardiman began to conduct research part-time at ICR in 1982, he had already spent almost ten years considering how the atmosphere may have been different before the Genesis Flood. He was interested in studying the conditions which would explain such things as a world-wide lack of rain before the Flood, no rainbows until after the Flood, and the longevity of the Patriarchs. At that time, he was working on a vapor canopy model which was intended to explain the source of a portion of the Flood waters. Using a numerical model developed by Dr. Joseph Dillow (1981), he was attempting to duplicate the results reported in, "*The Waters Above.*"

In 1987 David Rush (1990), an ICR graduate student, began work on this problem and helped develop a new one-dimensional, steady-state model which addressed the radiational issues of a large quantity of water vapor suspended in the upper atmosphere. It was built on the code called, LOWTRAN7, developed at the U.S. Air Force Cambridge Research Laboratory. The benefit of this approach was the application of a widely accepted radiation code to the canopy problem and a method for delimiting the amount of water the canopy could hold. This research is ongoing today because the model seems to indicate that no more than about 3 meters (~9 feet) of liquid water in vapor form could be held in such a canopy without producing an extreme greenhouse effect and heating the surface of the Earth to temperatures at which life as we know it could not exist.

In 1992 Dr. Vardiman turned a major portion of his attention to applying a 3-dimensional time-dependent global climate model to the "ice age" following the Flood. The reason for this change in direction from the canopy modeling was the apparently limited amount of water such a canopy can hold, but also, the recent findings by Wise, *et al.*(1994) that a catastrophic Flood probably disrupted the entire crust of the Earth creating the mid-ocean ridges and releasing large quantities of heat into the ocean during the Flood. Through the help of Herman Daily, a FORTRAN programmer retired from the Naval Weapons Center, Dr. Vardiman was able to adapt a global climate model to run on an IBM 486 PC. The original model called CCM1 was developed at the National Center for Atmospheric Research (NCAR) and routinely runs on a CRAY supercomputer. By limiting the size of some of the arrays and saving only selected output, the model was able to be run on a PC.

In 1994 Karen Spelman (1996), an ICR graduate student, began her thesis research on the effect of a uniform distribution of hot sea-surface temperatures on precipitation patterns using CCM1. She found that hot sea-surface temperatures energized the atmosphere producing stronger winds and more precipitation, particularly along continental boundaries and in polar regions. Many of the heavy precipitation regions were located in areas like Greenland and the North Atlantic Ocean where paleoclimatic evidence points toward high precipitation during the "ice age." The precipitation rates in some regions like Greenland indicated that the entire ice sheet present today could have accumulated in less than 500 years. Additional research with CCM1 showed that hot sea-surface temperatures over today's positions of the mid-ocean ridges gave very similar results to those of Spelman (1996).

In 1998 a mesoscale atmospheric model MM5 was explored for use with intense smaller-scale features like hurricanes which are believed to have been likely during the Genesis Flood and immediately following. This model, developed originally at The Pennsylvania State University and then implemented and supported at NCAR, was imported to ICR and operated on PCs. The model is a 3-dimensional time-dependent mesoscale model which draws on many standard data sources for input. The output can be animated in a 3-dimensional, colorized format using a display package called VIS5D.

In 1999 a case study was attempted by Nancy Zavacky, an ICR graduate student, on Hurricane Florence using MM5. Hurricane Florence occurred in the Gulf of Mexico in September, 1988. Sea-surface temperatures were increased above those observed during the hurricane in 10°C increments over the Gulf of Mexico and in a narrow band under the hurricane. These conditions would be similar to the hurricane being located over hot sea-surface conditions during and following the Flood. As expected, Hurricane Florence was energized by the hot sea-surface and spun up dramatically. The horizontal and vertical winds increased by 50% and 100%, respectively, and the precipitation rate increased by a factor of 10 for the hottest temperature simulated (45°C). Hotter temperatures were not possible because the model became unstable.

In addition to numerical model simulations, several analytic projects have been conducted on paleoclimate data, particularly on helium flux through the atmosphere, ice cores, and sea-floor sediment. In 1993 a monograph entitled, "Ice Cores and the Age of the Earth," was published by Dr. Vardiman (1993) after developing an analytic ice flow model for a young-earth time scale using the Camp Century ice core in Greenland. He found that it was possible to derive a theoretical, non steady-state, ice-flow equation which could have young-earth boundary conditions applied to it. During the development of the time scale for Camp Century it was found that a similar approach could be applied to the accumulation of sea-floor sediments. Vardiman (1996) published a monograph entitled, "Sea-floor Sediments and the Age of the Earth," reporting on a young-earth, deep sea-floor sediment time-scale.

Dr. Vardiman (1990) also published a monograph entitled, "The Age of the Earth's Atmosphere: A Study of Helium Flux through the Atmosphere." Dr. Harold Slusher, then chairman of the ICR Department of Astrogeophysics, had suggested the subject of helium escape several years before as a good evidence for a young earth because there was an apparent lack of helium in the atmosphere if the earth is billions of years old. Radioactive elements in the earth's crust release helium as a daughter product. If the earth's crust releases the helium to the atmosphere, there should be about 2 thousand times more helium in the atmosphere, even considering various mechanisms of escape of helium to space. The primary escape mechanism discussed in the monograph was thermal escape, first studied by James Jeans (1916) and later discounted as a sufficient loss mechanism by Cook (1957). Other escape mechanisms were discussed and also discounted in the monograph.

The conclusions of the helium flux study echo that of Walker and Hunten (1977) who said, ". . . there appears to be a problem with the helium budget of the atmosphere." Also, Chamberlain (1987) states that this helium escape problem, ". . . will not go away, and it is unsolved." The problem is only apparent if one holds that the earth and its atmosphere are billions of years old. If they are only thousands of years old, the problem goes away. Researchers working on this problem recently claimed that intermittent fluctuations in the temperature of earth's exosphere due to solar activity, large meteor bombardment of earth, or nearby supernovas would have allowed the helium to escape catastrophically. Yet, the evidence for such events are lacking - they are only conjectural. The conclusion of Vardiman (1990) that the earth must be young, still stands.

If the oxygen isotope record from cores in Greenland (Dansgaard, et al., 1971) are a true measure of the variation in the formation temperature of the snow over time, then an explanation needs to be developed for the slow trend toward more negative values of $\delta^{18}O$ in the lower part of the cores and the sudden increase near the top. The conventional explanation is that these trends occurred over a period of about 100,000 years and were induced by fluctuations in the orbital parameters of the Earth/Sun system. Dr. Vardiman has suggested a mechanism by which these same trends would occur in a period of about 5,000 years following the Genesis Flood. The mechanism he suggests is the slow formation of an ice shelf which covered the ocean surface as the oceans cooled during the "ice age" following the Genesis Flood. This movement of the source of water vapor from the open ocean to distances farther away from the site on Greenland where the snow was deposited and cores later drilled caused the $\delta^{18}O$ to decrease slowly. During the rapid deglaciation at the end of the "ice age" the source of water vapor moved rapidly closer to the core location reversing the trend rapidly. The dispersion of the different types and sizes of ice crystals formed in the storms near the edge of the ice shelf was the cause of the changing trends in $\delta^{18}O$. The results of this modeling effort were reported by Vardiman (1996) in a paper entitled, "Fractionation and Dispersion of Ice Crystals Near the Edge of an Ice Shelf During the Ice Age." Further studies of snow fall trajectories and precipitation accumulation are intended using the MM5 mesoscale model.

Some of the strongest evidence for the "ice age" is the coverage and movement of ice sheets and glaciers over the North American Continent. It appears that an ice sheet several thousand feet thick probably covered most of Canada, the northern U.S., and most mountain ranges in the western U.S. Preliminary calculations of precipitation rates and runoff from the Colorado River Basin have been made by Dr. Vardiman (2000) in a paper entitled, "Precipitation Rates and Runoff from the Colorado River Basin During the Ice Age." The large precipitation rates and runoff implied by the accumulation of large glaciers and ice sheets in Canada and over Yellowstone National Park during a young-Earth "ice age" imply significant contributions to the erosion of the Colorado River canyons and gorges and significant changes in the effective mountain topography and orographic cloud formation. The equivalent of 100 lakes the size of Lake Powell may have cascaded through the Grand Canyon during 100-300 years of deglaciation at the end of the "ice age." During the formation of the glaciers the mountains may have been 3-5,000 feet higher than they are today due to accumulated snow and ice. Further studies of orographic cloud formation and precipitation are intended using the MM5 mesoscale model.

In 1999 Jim Zavacky, an ICR graduate student, began using the latest data from the GISP2 ice core at Summit, Greenland to confirm the conclusions from Dr. Vardiman's (1993) earlier work on Camp Century. The GISP2 core is considerably longer, has many more measured variables than Camp Century, has better resolution, and is located nearer the ice divide, providing conditions which better satisfy flow model assumptions. He hopes to be able to confirm that the general procedures for developing a young-earth time scale are appropriate. He also hopes to be able to estimate the number of "annual layers" which appear to have formed each year as a function of depth. These "annual layers," are thought to actually be "storm layers," which increase in number with depth. There are estimated to be up to 6 storms layers per year at a depth of 1800 meters. Visible layers disappear below this level, so it is likely that snowfall was so heavy below this point that no layer formation occurred at all this far down.

One of the characteristic features of all ice cores in Greenland is a major disruption in the record of almost all measured variables at the "Younger Dryas." This strong signal occurs near the center of the deglaciation event, lasts 4 years or less, and is thought by most researchers to be a hint about the physical process which produced it. Because it is such a strong signal and occurs so rapidly, Steve Goodenow, another ICR graduate student, has taken on a project to explore this event and attempt to postulate a physical mechanism which might explain it and, at the same time, bolster the young-earth model. This type of open-ended research project may end in no progress or it could produce a major advance in the field. One principal of original research is to place a high priority on exploring strong signals. Generally, strong signals are produced by strong forcing functions and strong forcing functions should provide important hints about the mechanisms which are driving an unknown phenomenon. At this time, there is no fully-accepted model for the cause of the "ice ages" and their deglaciation. The best current explanation is the Astronomical Model, but it has major weaknesses and is intimately tied to the conventional old-Earth model. We need a superior young-earth explanation for the "ice age."

This monograph is intended to be a summary of the paleoclimate research conducted by Dr. Vardiman, his students, and associates at ICR over the past 20 years. Most of this research has already been published in various documents including monographs, journal articles, and conference proceedings. In addition to incorporating the major results, conclusions, and figures from all of the publications from this research program into this document, I also intend to discuss why each subproject was conducted and how they fit together into the bigger picture. It is also my intent to project what direction the research will take for the next ten years or so.

In writing this monograph it was surprising to realize how much ground had been covered and the level of effort at which it had been conducted. The Lord has provided the resources for this effort. Time and again He has made available computers, software, expert consultants, and students at exactly the right time to explore the research questions in the correct sequence. One example will suffice. In 1993 when the need to conduct global climate modeling became evident, the Lord provided four separate components to this project, all within a few months. The components were: 1) the concept of how to develop global climate modeling at ICR, 2) the gift of a high-end PC computer from employees of the Hewlett-Packard Corporation, 3) a free copy of the CCM1 code to ICR from the National Center for Atmospheric Research, and 4) the donated time by Herman Daily to convert the CCM1 code from a CRAY computer to a PC. The Lord also provided a supply of graduate students to work on many of these projects who had the skills and passion to work on the research. Many donors have also contributed funds to purchase computers, software, and supplies. It has been evident through the provision of these resources that the Lord is pleased to help ICR discover the "mysteries" of his activity in the atmosphere before, during, and following the Genesis Flood.

CHAPTER 2

A VAPOR CANOPY MODEL

Not long after graduating from Colorado State University with a Ph.D. in Atmospheric Science I received a call from Joseph Dillow, then a doctoral student at Dallas Theological Seminary, inquiring if I would be willing to assist him as a consultant on the research for his dissertation. He had been referred to me by Dr. Henry Morris. I had met Dr. Morris and Dr. Gish a few years earlier when they visited First Baptist Church of Ft. Collins, Colorado to present a creation seminar. I agreed to assist Dillow, although I was very busy working on other projects at the time.

Dillow was working on a dissertation project under the supervision of Dr. Charles Ryrie at Dallas. His topic was the Vapor Canopy. He was to complete a full expository study of the "waters" above the firmament, in what form they existed before the Genesis Flood, the effect they had on climate, and how they were removed during the Flood. He also included such topics as cultural mythology and the Flood, mammoths, estimates of changes in visibility with and without a canopy, and a model of the greenhouse effect under such a canopy.

My primary contribution was to advise him on the modeling of a vapor canopy and its effect on climate. This involvement with the vapor canopy was my first association with the creation movement. From about 1975 until 1980 I advised Dillow on his dissertation research and the conversion of his dissertation into a book entitled, "*The Waters Above*," which was published by Moody Press. The book was published in hardback and was revised once and printed a second time. In 1990 ICR obtained the rights to publish the book in paperback since Moody Press had decided to stop publishing it.

I contributed the analytic support for the distribution of water vapor with height in the atmosphere and an estimate of the diffusion rate of water vapor downward into the lower atmosphere. Dillow had earlier determined from his expository studies and general physical reasoning that the "waters above" were probably in vapor form and rested on top of today's atmosphere. He preferred a two-layer model of the atmosphere with pure water vapor above, resting on top of the air compressed below.

Dillow also assumed that the amount of water in vapor form in the canopy was a column equivalent to 40 feet of liquid water. He obtained this estimate from an assumed rainfall rate of 0.5 inches/hour over a period of 40 days and nights during the Flood. This rainfall rate would be considered to be a heavy rainfall rate today, particularly if it occurred uniformly over a large area. The Bible indicates that the rainfall was heavy during the first 40 days and nights of the Flood. If the quantity of water in the canopy was converted to rain over the entire earth during the 40 days and nights of the Flood, the canopy would have produced 40 feet of water on the ground.

Dillow also justified the 40 feet of water contained in his canopy by recognizing that the weight of water vapor in the canopy would increase the pressure of the atmosphere at the earth's surface. A column of water 34 feet high would produce one atmosphere of pressure at the bottom. So, 40 feet of water in the canopy on top of the air would increase the total pressure at the earth's surface to a little over two atmospheres. He had found that a pressure much greater than this would cause oxygen poisoning to human and animal life. So, these constraints seemed appropriate in estimating the amount of water in the canopy. In my modeling I chose to maintain 34 feet of water in the canopy to permit my pressure calculations, to be discussed later, to come out to one atmosphere at the base of the canopy and two atmospheres at the surface.

Because the vapor canopy would very effectively absorb infrared radiation coming upward from the surface of the earth and to a lesser degree some of the solar radiation coming down from above, it was assumed that the canopy would be hotter than the earth's surface. Under these conditions the change in temperature with altitude (lapse rate) in the lower atmosphere would be reversed from that experienced today. In other words, the temperature would increase with altitude from the earth's surface to the base of the canopy rather than decrease with altitude upwards as it normally does today.

Distribution of Water Vapor with Height

Figure 2.1 shows the distribution of temperature in the two-layer canopy model. I assumed a surface temperature of 30°C (90°F) and a temperature at the base of the canopy of 100°C (212°F). Because the weight of the overlying water vapor in the canopy compresses the air below, the base of the canopy and the top of the air layer, was found to occur at about 7 kilometers. This creates a change in temperature with altitude below the canopy of 70°C over a distance of 7 kilometers or 10°C/km. From the base of the canopy upward I assumed the change of temperature with altitude to decrease at a rate of 1°C/km. Given these conditions I was able to derive the pressure in the atmosphere as a function of altitude.

Two additional assumptions are needed to complete this derivation, both of which are commonly made in today's atmosphere. The first is that air and water vapor follow the ideal gas law. This is easily demonstrated for air at temperatures commonly encountered in the atmosphere, but is only true for water vapor when the temperature is far from the triple point (the temperature and pressure at which the three phases of a substance - solid, liquid, and gas - can exist simultaneously in equilibrium). Although we will encounter temperatures at or near the triple point high in the canopy, we will still assume that water vapor follows the idea gas law to maintain a simple analytic solution. Our main focus will be lower in the atmosphere where the temperatures are far from the triple point. The ideal gas law may be stated as follows:

$$P = \rho R T \tag{2.1}$$

where P is pressure in millibars, ρ is density in moles/meter^3, R is the universal gas constant equal to 0.287 Joules/mole K, and T is temperature in degrees Kelvin, K.

The second assumption is that gravity is constant through the thin layer of the atmosphere and the hydrostatic equation holds as follows:

$$\frac{dP}{dz} = -\rho g \tag{2.2}$$

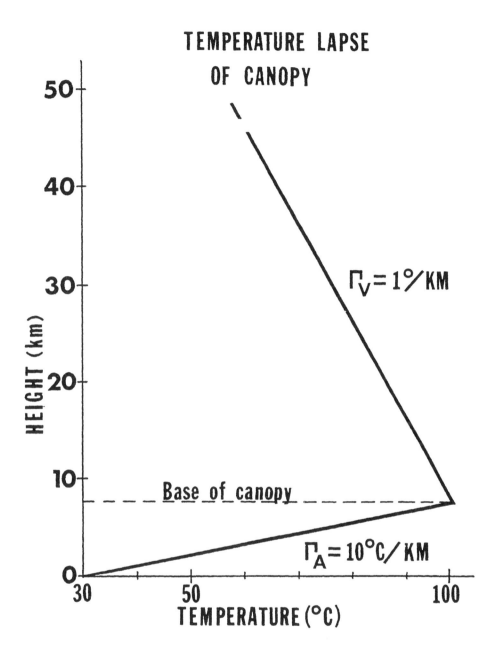

Figure 2.1 Temperature as a function of altitude for a two-layer atmosphere in the vapor canopy model. The upper layer is all water vapor and the lower layer is air.

Solving Eq. 2.1 for ρ and substituting into Eq. 2.2 gives:

$$\frac{dP}{dz} = -\frac{Pg}{RT} \qquad (2.3)$$

Separating variables:

$$\frac{dP}{P} = -\frac{gdz}{RT} \qquad (2.4)$$

We wish to find pressure, P, as a function of altitude, z, in two layers as shown in Fig. 2.1. If we assume that temperature, T, increases linearly from the surface of the earth where the pressure is $2P_o$ and the altitude is 0, to the base of the canopy where the pressure is P_o and the altitude is z, T may be written:

$$T = T_o - \gamma z \qquad (2.5)$$

where T_o is the temperature at the earth's surface and γ is the lapse rate. γ is defined as $-dT/dZ$ and is positive in the troposphere today. Substituting Eq. 2.5 into Eq. 2.4 gives:

$$\frac{dP}{P} = -\frac{gdz}{R(T_o-\gamma z)} \qquad (2.6)$$

Since g, $R=R_d$(dry air), T_o, and $\gamma=\gamma_d=-10°K/km$ are all constant in the lower air layer of Fig. 2.1, Eq. 2.6 can be integrated for pressure from $2P_o$ to P and z from 0 to z according to a standard differential formula to give:

$$P = 2P_o \left(\frac{T_o-\gamma_d z}{T_o}\right)^{\frac{g}{R_d \gamma_d}} \qquad (2.7)$$

Similarly, Eq. 2.6 can be integrated for pressure from P_o to P and altitude from z_v(altitude of the vapor canopy base) to z where g, $R=R_v$(vapor), T_o, and $\gamma_v=1°K/km$ are all constants in the upper vapor canopy layer to give:

$$P = P_o \left(\frac{T_o-\gamma_v z}{T_o}\right)^{\frac{g}{R_v \gamma_v}} \qquad (2.8)$$

Fig. 2.2 shows pressure plotted as a function of altitude from Eqs. 2.7 and 2.8 for the two layers in Fig. 2.1. Notice that the curves are logarithmic in both layers. A cusp is evident at the base of the canopy where the gas changes from air to water vapor but pressure is continuous at one atmosphere. The change in slope enters the equations through the different values of the gas constant, R.

A plot of saturation vapor pressure as a function of the temperature at each level in the atmosphere for water is also shown in Fig. 2.2. Notice that in the upper canopy layer the actual vapor pressure is less than the saturation vapor pressure except at the very top of the atmosphere and at the base of the canopy. This is good, because wherever the actual vapor pressure exceeds the saturation vapor pressure, liquid water would condense out and the canopy collapse. In fact, unless the temperature at the canopy base is not maintained at a high enough temperature, the

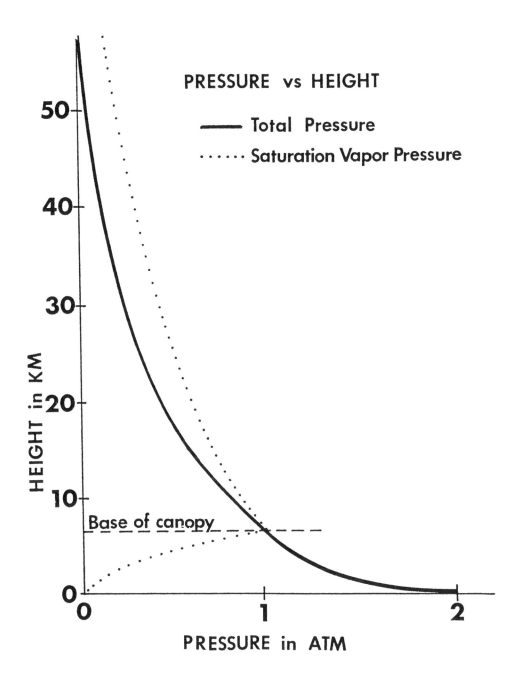

Figure 2.2 Pressure as a function of altitude in a two-layer vapor canopy model. The solid line is pressure and the dashed line is saturation vapor pressure.

canopy will collapse at the bottom. The pressure at any point in the canopy is due to the weight of the overlying water vapor. So, condensation and rain will occur until the weight above has been reduced so that the actual vapor pressure is less than the saturation vapor pressure.

At the top of the atmosphere the temperature will eventually become cold enough that the vapor pressure exceeds the saturation vapor pressure. Fortunately for the vapor canopy model this only introduces a minor convective cell near the top of the atmosphere. Results of more refined modeling later will show that this cell occurs at cold temperatures where snow forms and precipitates. The precipitation falls to lower levels in the canopy where it re-evaporates causing layers of water vapor above to be lifted upward replacing the condensed vapor. This continually overturning cell produces a cirrus cloud near the top of the atmosphere which remains suspended. This cell not only conserves the mass of water vapor, it may also dramatically influence the radiation balance of the entire vapor canopy system.

Because the temperature decreases rapidly toward lower levels in the atmosphere beneath the canopy base, any water vapor which diffuses downward into the lower layer will likely be condensed out as rain and fall, moistening the lower atmosphere. As long as the diffusion of water vapor downward through the cloud base is small, the loss will be small. But this loss can never be returned to the canopy because the colder temperatures at the earth's surface and in the lower layer act as a vapor sink. Only if temperatures were maintained higher than the canopy base somewhere on the earth could water vapor be transported upward. Consequently, once the canopy collapses it will not be reformed naturally.

Diffusion of Water Vapor Downward

One of the immediate concerns which was raised soon after the vapor canopy model was developed was, "How stable is it?" The Bible indicates that the canopy probably existed from day 2 of the creation week to part way through the Flood. Ussher's chronology would estimate this period of time to be about 1,656 years. What about the diffusion of water vapor downward to the lower atmosphere and condensation into rain? Even a small rate of diffusion would deplete the mass of water vapor in the canopy over such a long time.

There are two types of diffusion of water vapor which would likely occur in such an atmosphere - molecular diffusion and eddy diffusion. Molecular diffusion is the movement of water vapor through the canopy base into the air below by the random collision of individual molecules. Eddy diffusion is the movement of water vapor by the organized circulation of air which exchanges large numbers of water molecules. Molecular diffusion normally occurs very slowly and is proportional to the temperature of the system and the concentration gradient of the two species which are diffusing through each other. Eddy diffusion may occur rapidly if convective instability and/or wind shear is present to drive the eddies. However, it is likely that under the extremely stable atmospheric conditions in and below the vapor canopy, eddy diffusion was practically nonexistent. Even if it did exist, eddy diffusion is difficult to quantify. An attempt was made to estimate the rate of molecular diffusion downward which may have existed in a vapor canopy.

Molecular diffusion in gases is governed by Fick's Law which states that:

$$\frac{dM}{dt} = -DA\frac{d\rho}{dz} \qquad (2.9)$$

where dM/dt is the differential mass of water vapor diffused normal to a unit area, A, per unit time, t, D is the diffusivity, and $d\rho/dz$ is the gradient of molecular density per unit distance normal to the unit area. The diffusivity, D, is a function of temperature and pressure, as follows:

$$D = D_o\left(\frac{T}{T_o}\right)^{1.81}\left(\frac{P_o}{P}\right) \qquad (2.10)$$

where D is the diffusivity in cm^2/sec at pressure, P, and temperature, T, and D_o is the diffusivity at $T_o = 0°C$ (+32°F) and $P_o = 1000$ mb.

Substituting Eqs. 2.5 and 2.7 into Eq. 2.10 and then 2.10 into Eq. 2.9 gives the following relationship for the rate of diffusion rate of water vapor into the lower layer of the model atmosphere:

$$\frac{dM}{dt} = -D_o\left(\frac{T_o+\gamma_d z}{T_o}\right)^{1.81}\left[\frac{P_o}{P_o\left(\frac{T_o+\gamma_d z}{T_o}\right)^{\frac{g}{R_d\gamma_d}}}\right]A\frac{d\rho}{dz} \qquad (2.11)$$

Equation 2.11 can be solved numerically for a time-dependent situation in the vapor canopy by forming thin horizontal layers, calculating the vertical density gradient of water vapor, substituting the temperature at each layer, and calculating the diffusion rate as a function of time. Fig. 2.3 shows such a diffusion scheme with 70 horizontal layers of 100 meters thickness and 71 levels beneath the vapor canopy base. The first time step in the numerical calculation of the diffusion causes water vapor to diffuse rapidly downward into the first layer beneath the canopy base because the gradient is artificially large. No water vapor is assumed to be present in any of the layers below the canopy base initially. At the second time step, water vapor will diffuse rapidly into the second layer below the canopy base, and so on. Once all the layers have some water vapor in them, the diffusion rate downward will decrease rapidly.

Fig. 2.4 shows the rate of diffusion of water vapor downward (cm/year of equivalent water thickness) into the first layer below the vapor canopy base. The amount and rate of water vapor diffusing through this layer is directly related to the amount of water vapor in the canopy above and the amount in the layers beneath the canopy. Notice that the rate of diffusion is rapid at first but decreases very quickly. The total mass of water vapor which would diffuse through this layer over the first year is less than about 1 cm. Over 10 years it is about 6 cm. Over 100 years it is about 25 cm. The diffusion rate is extremely small by 1,656 years and the total amount diffused by that time is about 100 cm, only 9% of the total of 34 feet which was in the canopy initially. This amount is probably an overestimate because most of it occurred during the initial 70 time steps when the layers were being filled with water vapor. Therefore, it can be concluded that molecular diffusion is not likely to remove a significant quantity of water vapor from a vapor canopy.

P(mb)	T(K)	H(km)	Level(i)	Layer(j)
1013	400.0	7.0 ———————————————— 1		
				1
1022	398.6	6.9 ———————————————— 2		
				2
1031	397.1	6.8 ———————————————— 3		
				3
1040	395.7	6.7 ———————————————— 4		
				4
1049	394.3	6.6 ———————————————— 5		
		⋮		
1982	302.8	0.2 ———————————————— 69		
				69
2004	301.4	0.1 ———————————————— 70		
				70
2026	300.0	0.0 ———————————————— 71		

Figure 2.3 Schematic of layers in canopy model through which water vapor diffuses downward.

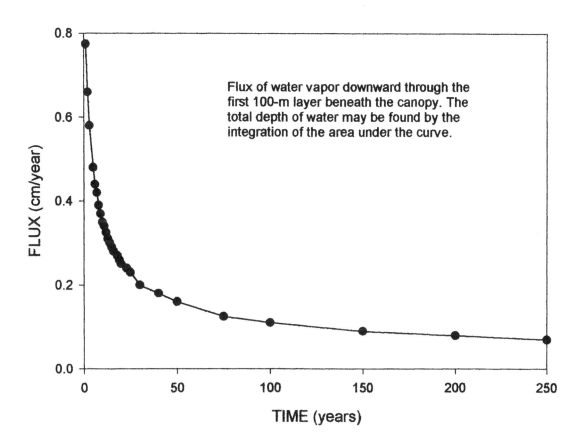

Figure 2.4 Rate of diffusion of water vapor downward with time through the first layer below the base of the canopy.

Radiational Properties of a Vapor Canopy

Although it was well known that water vapor is generally a poor absorber of short-wave radiation from the sun and it was known that water vapor is a good absorber of infrared radiation from the earth at concentrations commonly observed in the atmosphere today, it was not known what the radiational properties of an atmosphere would be with such large quantities of water vapor as that suggested by Dillow (1981). Of most interest were two questions: (1) Could water vapor canopies of different magnitude be maintained in radiational balance without collapsing? and (2) Would surface temperature conditions be livable under such extreme greenhouse conditions?

Rush (1990) began his Masters thesis research at the ICR Graduate School in 1987 and, to a large degree, answered these two questions. Rush (1990) used a state-of-the-art radiation program to build a one-dimensional, steady-state canopy model. He constructed several multi-level distributions of water vapor in a two-layer atmosphere similar to that suggested by Dillow (1981). The model contained parameters such as the solar constant and the earth's albedo which were set to values observed today. He began a model run with a uniform vertical temperature distribution of 170°K (-150°F) and allowed the radiational properties of LOWTRAN, a radiation code developed by the U.S. Air Force Cambridge Research Laboratories, to heat the model atmosphere until it came to equilibrium.

Rush (1990) was able to duplicate the average vertical temperature distribution in today's atmosphere when he selected the typical distribution of water vapor. He then selected four distributions of water vapor for canopies which contained the equivalent of 4 inches, 20 inches, 40 inches, and 34 feet of liquid water. He found that in all four cases the atmosphere warmed to the point where the water vapor in the canopy was maintained in the vapor state. Fig. 2.5 shows the vertical temperature distribution of a vapor canopy with the equivalent of 20 inches of water as it warms from an initial uniform temperature of 170°K. Notice that the warming slows as the equilibrium temperature is approached. Also, note the canopy base at the break in the temperature distribution about half way up. The upper part of the atmosphere in this simulation warms more quickly than the lower part because water vapor is more radiationally active than air. The more water vapor present in the canopy, the higher the equilibrium temperature became, such that, the vapor pressure was always higher than the saturation vapor pressure. So, the first question was answered in the affirmative. It appeared that vapor canopies of any magnitude could be maintained by solar radiation.

However, the answer to the second question seemed to indicate that only thin vapor canopies would allow livable conditions on earth's surface. Fig. 2.6 shows the equilibrium temperature at the surface of the earth for canopies with various amounts of water equivalent. Any canopy which contained more than about 20 inches of water produced such a strong greenhouse effect that surface temperatures became unsuitable for life. Rush and Vardiman's (1990) conclusion was tempered by the finding that a cirrus cloud could form near the top of the canopy and possibly affect the radiational properties of the entire canopy. However, the greenhouse effect seemed so strong that they were dubious about the cirrus cloud changing this conclusion significantly.

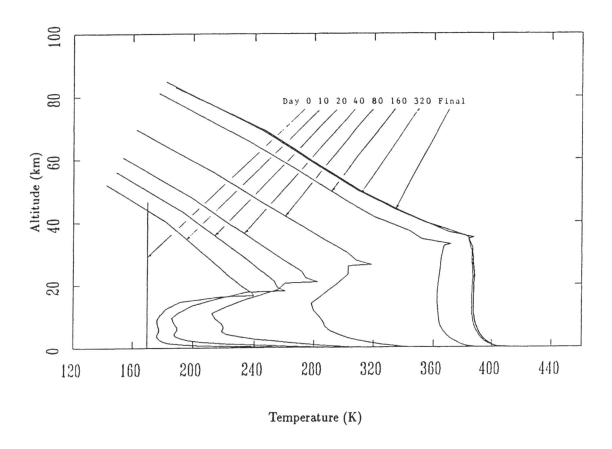

Figure 2.5 Vertical temperature distributions as a function of time for a vapor canopy with the equivalent of 20 inches of water. The vertical line at 170 K is the uniform initial temperature throughout the canopy and the other curves are at the indicated number of days after radiational heating was begun. The final curve is at equilibrium when temperature changes ceased.

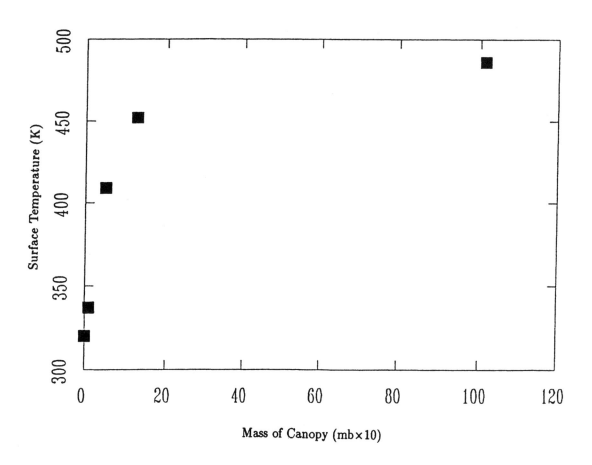

Figure 2.6 Equilibrium temperatures for various canopies with different quantities of equivalent amounts of water.

The magnitude of the greenhouse effect uncovered by Rush and Vardiman (1990) was a great disappointment to many canopy advocates. If the canopy could only hold 20 inches of water or less, it would not have contributed greatly to the Genesis Flood. I had assumed before starting the canopy modeling that it could have contributed as much as half of the waters of the Flood. However, with each step in the research the contribution had dropped significantly. It is now obvious that if the vapor canopy existed, it would have only contributed a small portion of the Flood water. On the other hand, even 20 inches of water in a canopy would have caused major changes to the earth's climate. Evidence of past climatic change might justify continued work on the vapor canopy model even if it is not a major source of Flood water.

Sensitivity Studies of a Vapor Canopy Model

In hopes of increasing the quantity of water a canopy could hold and still allow surface temperatures to be livable, a sensitivity study was conducted on some of the "constants" used in the canopy model. Five constants in the radiation model developed by Rush and Vardiman (1990) were originally set at fixed values typical of today's atmosphere. The constants and their values were:

Solar constant (rate of heating of the earth by the sun) - 2 calories/cm^2/min
Albedo (average percent of reflected energy from the earth's surface) - 13%
Solar zenith angle (angle of the sun from the vertical) - 60°
Cirrus cloud height (height of thin cloud of ice crystals) - no cloud
Cirrus cloud thickness (vertical thickness of thin cloud of ice crystals) - no cloud

It would appear that other geometry or physical conditions must have been present before the Flood for a vapor canopy to have contained enough water to contribute significantly to the Genesis Flood. Before considering more exotic water vapor distributions such as an elevated shell of water vapor surrounding the earth not in contact with the lower atmosphere, it was thought advisable to explore the effects of varying some of the constants used in radiation models. This exploration will determine the sensitivity of surface temperature to variations in factors other than water vapor content.

The same 10 millibar canopy model used by Rush and Vardiman (1990) was used for this study. All other constants were maintained at the original values while a single constant was varied. Table 2.1 shows the ranges over which the 5 constants were varied.

In each model run the atmosphere was allowed to come to equilibrium so that the temperature at all levels remained uniform with time. Fig. 2.7 shows an example of the equilibrium profiles reached for the various values of the Solar Constant. Similar profiles were obtained by varying the other parameters. From these profiles, temperatures at various levels in the atmosphere were plotted as a function of the value of the constant.

Table 2.1 Normal values and their ranges used for the constants in the sensitivity study.

Constant	Normal Value	Minimum Value	Maximum Value
Solar Constant (Cal/cm^2/min)	2	0.5	4.0
Albedo (%)	13	0	25
Solar Zenith Angle (°)	60	0	75
Cloud Thickness (km)	No Cloud	0	10
Cloud Base Height (km)	No Cloud	0	50

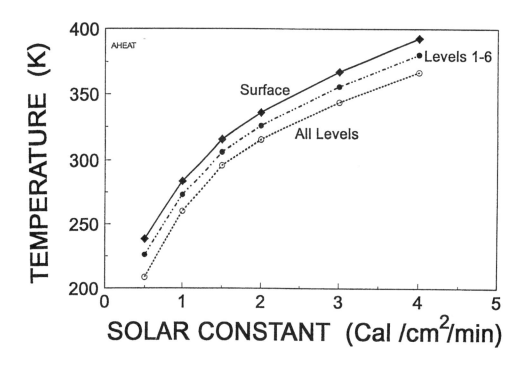

Figure 2.7 Equilibrium temperature distributions as a function of solar constant.

Surface temperatures were most strongly affected by changes in the solar constant. A 50% reduction in the solar constant reduced the surface temperature under the canopy from 335K (+140°F) to 240K (-25°F). The albedo, solar zenith angle, and cirrus cloud thickness also produced strong effects on surface temperature. However, none of the effects were so dramatic that the concern over limitations on water content in the canopy by hot surface temperatures was eliminated. If all five parameters were introduced into the model simultaneously such that the surface temperature was minimized, it is estimated that the water content of the canopy could possibly be raised to as much as 1.0 meter. This is less than 10% of the water content suggested by Dillow (1981). Unfortunately, this amount of water in a canopy would not contribute significantly to the waters of the Genesis Flood or produce important pressure and density effects. However, it would produce large differences in temperature, atmospheric stability, cloud formation, and precipitation from that experienced today.

Although this result is disappointing for advocates of a vapor canopy, the story may not yet be complete. It is possible that the high albedo produced at the top of a cloud layer in the canopy may reduce the flux of radiation into the canopy and atmosphere greatly reducing the heating. This effect was not included in the simulations by Vardiman and Bousselot [formerly Spelman] (1998) except possibly through the reduction in solar constant. The albedo changes modeled were only due to those effects at the surface of the earth.

It is recommended that a simulation be conducted where all five "constants" are held at the values where the surface temperature is minimized simultaneously and the albedo effect at the top of the clouds in the canopy be included to determine the maximum amount of water vapor the canopy can hold. It is also recommended that the complex relationship between cloud thickness, cloud base height, and vertical temperature profiles be explored farther. Three dimensional global circulation models (GCMs) should be used to simulate the affect of varying the albedo and solar zenith angle under the canopy. GCMs are designed to compute the global circulation caused by varying three dimensional patterns of albedo and solar geometry.

If these efforts fail to permit a sizable quantity of water to be maintained in the canopy, then consideration should be given to exploring canopies in orbits above the atmosphere where thermodynamic considerations do not constrain the quantity of water.

CHAPTER 3

HELIUM ESCAPE FROM THE ATMOSPHERE

Introduction

For several years it has been recognized that the concentration of helium in the atmosphere is not as great as it should be if the earth is billions of years old (Cook, 1957). The crust of the earth contains large concentrations of radioactive uranium and other elements which produce helium as daughter products when they decay. This helium escapes from the crust and diffuses upward into the atmosphere where a large majority of it is trapped. If this decay and diffusion has been going on for millions of years, the atmosphere should have about 2 thousand times more helium than it has today.

This is a good argument for a young earth. Of course, many would question this conclusion because they believe there must be one or more mechanisms for the escape of helium from the atmosphere which would explain this discrepancy. In fact, helium does escape from the atmosphere by several processes; thermal escape, polar wind escape, solar wind sweeping, hot-ion exchange, or meteoroid bombardment being the most commonly suggested mechanisms. Through 1990, however, none of these mechanisms had been shown to be an adequate process by which the deficit in helium could be explained.

This chapter will treat the theoretical development of the thermal escape of helium and briefly discuss other mechanisms. A more complete treatment may be found in Vardiman (1990). An updated review of the literature is needed to find out if the situation has changed since 1990, particularly on polar wind escape and solar wind sweeping.

Thermal Escape of Helium

The earth's atmosphere is predominantly nitrogen (78%) and oxygen (21%). It also contains many other minor constituents. Table 1 show the composition of the atmosphere at ground level, given by Walker (1977). With the exception of water vapor, soluble gases, and particulates, the atmosphere below 100 kilometers is quite well mixed. Variations in the concentration of the major components are slight. Large deviations from the near-suface composition are confined to heights near and above 100 kilometers. Between 100 and 800 kilometers, molecular oxygen is dissociated into atomic oxygen and becomes the most important neutral gas. Above 800 kilometers, helium becomes the most abundant element. Finally, hydrogen predominates in the region where the earth's atmosphere merges with interplanetary space.

Of the gases listed in Table 1, Argon, Neon, Helium, Krypton, and Xenon are of most interest in questions regarding the age of the earth. This is due to the fact that they are noble gases which do not chemically react with other elements. Therefore, the quantity of these gases present in today's atmosphere should be related to the age of the earth, if the rate of their production and/or loss to space can be calculated. Argon is an important gas because it is present in relatively large quantities and is sufficiently heavy that it does not escape the earth's gravitational pull. It can be used as an upper limit for the production of atmospheric gases by radioactive decay. Helium occurs in two isotope forms ^{3}He and ^{4}He. Both are light enough that they can escape to space to some degree, but at slightly different rates. Their diffusion rates through the lower atmosphere, however, are approximately the same magnitude. The total mass of ^{4}He in the atmosphere is 3.8×10^{15} gm, or about 6×10^{38} atoms. The total mass of ^{3}He is 5.3×10^9 gm or about 1×10^{33} atoms. The mass ratio of ^{3}He to ^{4}He in the atmosphere today is 1.4×10^{-6}.

Table 3.1   Composition of the atmosphere [after Walker (1977)].

Constituent	Chemical Formula	Molecular Weight (^{12}C = 12)	Percent by Volume in Dry Air	Total Mass (gm)
Total Atmosphere				$(5.136 \pm 0.007) \times 10^{21}$
Water Vapor	H_2O	18.01534	Variable	$(0.017 \pm 0.001) \times 10^{21}$
Dry Air		28.9644	100.0	$(5.119 \pm 0.008) \times 10^{21}$
Nitrogen	N_2	28.0134	78.084 ± 0.004	$(3.866 \pm 0.006) \times 10^{21}$
Oxygen	O_2	31.9988	20.948 ± 0.002	$(1.185 \pm 0.002) \times 10^{21}$
Argon	Ar	39.948	$0.934 \pm .001$	$(6.59 \pm 0.01) \times 10^{19}$
Carbon Dioxide	CO_2	44.00995	0.0315 ± 0.0010	$(2.45 \pm 0.08) \times 10^{18}$
Neon	Ne	20.183	$(1.818 \pm 0.004) \times 10^{-3}$	$(6.48 \pm 0.02) \times 10^{16}$
Helium	He	4.0026	$(5.24 \pm 0.05) \times 10^{-4}$	$(3.71 \pm 0.04) \times 10^{15}$
Krypton	Kr	83.80	$(1.14 \pm 0.01) \times 10^{-4}$	$(1.69 \pm 0.02) \times 10^{16}$
Xenon	Xe	131.30	$(8.7 \pm 0.1) \times 10^{-6}$	$(2.02 \pm 0.02) \times 10^{15}$
Methane	CH_4	16.04303	$\sim 1.5 \times 10^{-4}$	$\sim 4.3 \times 10^{15}$
Hydrogen	H_2	2.01594	$\sim 5 \times 10^{-5}$	$\sim 1.8 \times 10^{14}$
Nitrous Oxide	N_2O	44.0128	$\sim 3 \times 10^{-5}$	$\sim 2.3 \times 10^{15}$
Carbon Monoxide	CO	28.0106	$\sim 1.2 \times 10^{-5}$	$\sim 5.9 \times 10^{14}$
Ammonia	NH_3	17.0306	$\sim 1 \times 10^{-6}$	$\sim 3 \times 10^{13}$
Nitrogen Dioxide	NO_2	46.0055	$\sim 1 \times 10^{-7}$	$\sim 8.1 \times 10^{12}$
Sulfur Dioxide	SO_2	64.063	$\sim 2 \times 10^{-8}$	$\sim 2.3 \times 10^{12}$
Hydrogen Sulfide	H_2S	34.080	$\sim 2 \times 10^{-8}$	$\sim 1.2 \times 10^{12}$
Ozone	O_3	47.9982	Variable	$\sim 3.3 \times 10^{15}$

The two isotopes of helium in the atmosphere may be traced to several sources. The first source is primordial helium. That is, the helium we observe may have been present at the time the atmosphere was formed. Since no observations of the initial conditions are available, whether the atmosphere was formed a few thousand years ago or several billion, we cannot know the original quantity of helium. The old-earth model speculates that there was no helium initially, because the atmosphere was yet to form. The young-earth model, on the other hand, would suggest that the initial conditions were very similar to those of today, although changes in the helium concentration may have occurred since the creation of the atmosphere. It is also possible that significant changes could have occurred during creation week, during the judgment in the Garden of Eden, or during the Flood. A group of young-earth creationists working on RATE (Radioisotopes and the Age of the Earth) are currently exploring this possibility. They have proposed as one of their research hypotheses that God may have accelerated the decay rate of the radioactive isotopes for a period of time, creating a large pulse of gaseous daughter products like Argon and Helium. The RATE group hopes to report their results in 2005 after a 5-year period of research.

The old-earth model has, for many years, assumed no primordial helium in the earth or atmosphere. However, the recent discovery by Clarke *et al.* (1969) of ^{3}He leaking through the crust has forced the recognition of primordial helium in the mantle. This admission was necessary because no known radioactive decay process in the mantle is known to produce ^{3}He. It is now recognized that at least a small portion of the ^{4}He may also be primordial. The question then arises, if primordial helium can exist in the mantle, why could it not have also existed in the atmosphere when it was formed? Of course, we can still assume that no helium existed initially, and use the current process rates to calculate a maximum age. We will make these calculations for comparative purposes, but we must always remember that the amount of primordial helium could reduce the age significantly. Putting aside the question of primordial helium, let's consider other sources of helium observed today. These sources can best be described if the two isotopes are considered separately.

The radioactive decay of uranium (^{235}U and ^{238}U) and thorium (^{232}Th) results in the formation of helium (^{4}He) as a by-product. Since the crust of the earth contains a large, unknown quantity of these elements, the crust is generally agreed to be the major source of ^{4}He for the atmosphere. ^{4}He is produced in the crust, seeps to the surface, and mixes through the atmosphere. At the same time Argon (^{40}Ar) is produced in the radioactive decay of potassium (^{40}K). Wasserburg (1963) found that the atomic ratio of ^{4}He to radiogenic ^{40}Ar is between 0.2 and 5 in many samples of natural gas. It is commonly assumed that the mean value of the ^{4}He/^{40}Ar ratio in gases entering the atmosphere is on the order of unity; yet the ^{4}He/^{40}Ar ratio in the atmosphere is only 1/1800. If ^{40}Ar is too heavy to escape, and both ^{4}He and ^{40}Ar only enter the atmosphere by this process, then ^{4}He must be escaping from the atmosphere. Assuming that the number of ^{4}He atoms that have entered the atmosphere is the same as the number of ^{40}Ar atoms, the residence time for ^{4}He entering the atmosphere is approximately 2 million years. Residence time is defined as the total amount of gas present, divided by the rate of net inflow or outflow. The total number of atoms of ^{4}He in the atmosphere is about 6×10^{38} and the rate of inflow over the entire surface of the earth is estimated to be about 2×10^6 atoms/cm^2/sec.

Efforts to calculate the rate of flow of ^{4}He from the crust of the earth to the atmosphere in other ways have met with limited success. First, it is difficult to measure the flow of such small quantities of a gas through an average crustal interface. Secondly, the actual flow of helium seems to be concentrated in certain locations, such as near fumeroles, in volcanoes, at the mid-oceanic rise, etc. The calculation of an average rate of flow based on non-homogeneous time and space releases leads to large errors. Thirdly, a direct calculation of radioactive decay rates is dependent upon an unknown distribution of uranium and thorium in the crust and mantle. Attempts have been made to improve such compositional models of the earth, using measurements of heat flow caused by radioactive decay. However, these computations are difficult, at best, and are suspect because of assumptions made in handling the initial heat of formation of the earth and the long-age time frame. Again, it is necessary to point out that the assumptions of no original helium and a 4.5 billion-year age for the earth are implicit in the conclusion that 6×10^{38} ^{4}He atoms entered the atmosphere at a rate of 2×10^6 atoms/cm^2/sec. The same rate could have been calculated assuming only 6×10^{32} ^{4}He atoms entered the atmosphere over a period of 4,500 years.

It was assumed, until 1969, that the primary source of ^{3}He to the atmosphere was the production of tritium by cosmic bombardment of nitrogen in the upper atmosphere, and its subsequent decay to ^{3}He. A second source was assumed to be direct injection of ^{3}He by the solar wind. These production rates were relatively small, amounting to about 0.5 atoms/cm^2/sec, as reported by Craig and Lal (1961). Clarke *et al.* (1969) reported the occurrence of excess ^{3}He in the ocean, which they interpreted as evidence for terrestrial primordial helium trapped in the mantle. Lupton and Craig (1975), Craig *et al.* (1975), Craig and Lupton (1976), Rison and Craig (1983), and Welhan and Craig (1983) subsequently traced the excess ^{3}He in the ocean to releases from the mantle. Since there are no radiogenic sources of ^{3}He in the mantle, this was direct evidence for primordial helium. Through this effort, evidence for some primordial ^{4}He was also discovered. Craig *et al.* (1975) estimated the total flux of ^{3}He to the atmosphere from all sources to be about 4.6 atoms/cm^2/sec. The residence time for ^{3}He, given that the quantity of ^{3}He in today's atmosphere is 1×10^{33} atoms, is about 1 million years.

According to the old-earth model the average flow rate of ^{4}He flow from the crust of the earth to the atmosphere of 2×10^6 atoms/cm^2/sec over a period of 4.5 billion years should have provided a total mass of helium to the atmosphere of 7.3×10^{18} gm. This is about 2000 times the quantity of 3.8×10^{15} grams actually measured. According to the old-age model a significant loss of ^{4}He must have occurred. The main loss mechanism considered by Vardiman (1990) to explain this discrepancy was thermal escape of gases from a planet theorized by Jeans (1916). We will describe this theory in considerable detail, since it has played such an important role in this problem.

The density of the atmosphere decreases with height. At some level, the mean free path (the average distance between collisions) of the constituent particles becomes large in comparison with the scale height of the atmosphere (the equivalent depth of an incompressible atmosphere) and collisions above this level are infrequent. Scale height may be defined in other words as the thickness of an equivalent homogeneous atmosphere with constant density. The region high in the atmosphere in which collisions are negligible is termed the exosphere. The atmosphere grades into the exosphere; however, for the purposes of escape theory, it is usual to speak of a given level as the base of the exosphere. Below this level, collisions are frequent enough that the particles assume a Maxwellian velocity distribution (see Fig. 3.4). From the base of the exosphere, some particles are ejected upward with velocities less than that required for escape. These particles describe elliptic, ballistic orbits and return to the base of the exosphere. Some fraction of the particles describing ballistic orbits have a velocity greater than the escape velocity. These particles will leave the exosphere in hyperbolic orbits. In addition, there is a component in elliptical orbits circling the planet and not passing through regions where the density is high enough for collisions to take place.

A basic question in the theory of planetary escape is the calculation of the fraction of atoms which have a velocity such that their kinetic energy is greater than the gravitational potential energy. The classical theory of escape was developed by Jeans (1916) and Lennard-Jones (1923). These models assumed an isothermal atmosphere with a gas in equilibrium having a Maxwellian velocity distribution up to the base of the exosphere. Above this level, collisions are sufficiently infrequent as to be unimportant in slowing down outward traveling particles. A refinement that has influenced much of the later work is given by Spitzer (1949). His model considered the changes to the Maxwellian velocity distribution below the exosphere, as the high energy particles were removed by escape. MacDonald (1964) summarized the theory of thermal escape and applied it specifically to the escape of helium from the earth's atmosphere. This discussion will largely follow his treatment. The problem of escape is complicated by the fact that for a minor constituent, the base of the exosphere must be supplied through diffusion from below. If the thermal conditions are such that the escape rate of a particular constituent is large compared with the diffusion rate, then diffusion effectively controls the escape of that constituent. If the escape rate is small compared to the diffusion rate, then the rate of escape is the controlling factor. It appears that the latter case is normally true for helium, although during unusual events such as solar storms, when the exosphere is strongly heated, the diffusion rate from below may control the flux of helium.

It is usual to assume that the distribution of atmospheric pressure with height obeys the hydrostatic law,

$$\frac{dP}{dz} = -\rho g \qquad 3.1$$

where P is the total pressure, z is the height above the surface, ρ is the density, and g is the acceleration due to gravity. both pressure and density are functions of time and height. The acceleration due to gravity also varies with height at altitudes considered in the escape of helium. Eq. 3.1 describes what is called hydrostatic equilibrium.

Density is a function of the number density or concentration of the constituents, n_i, and the molecular masses, m_i:

$$\rho = \sum_i m_i n_i \qquad 3.2$$

It is also assumed that the atmosphere behaves like a perfect gas with the equation of state:

$$P = nkT \qquad 3.3$$

where k is the Boltzman constant (1.38×10^{-16} ergs K^{-1}), T is the absolute temperature, and n is the total number concentration.

$$n = \sum_i n_i \qquad 3.4$$

where the summation is over all the constituents, i. From Eq. 3.3 we see that the vertical variation of pressure depends on the local values of number concentration and temperature, and on the gradients of concentration and temperature as follows:

$$\frac{dP}{dz} = kT\frac{dn}{dz} + kn\frac{dT}{dz} \qquad 3.5$$

Combining Eqs. 3.1 and 3.5, we see that the number concentration gradient depends on the local values of temperature, number concentration, density, and temperature gradient.

$$\frac{dn}{dz} = -\frac{\rho g}{kT} - \frac{n}{T}\frac{dT}{dz} \qquad 3.6$$

Substituting Eq. 3.2 into 3.7:

$$\frac{dn}{dz} = -\frac{\sum_i m_i n_i g}{kT} - \frac{n}{T}\frac{dT}{dz} \qquad 3.7$$

And, substituting Eq. 3.4 into 3.7:

$$\frac{d(\sum_i n_i)}{dz} = -\frac{\sum_i m_i n_i g}{kT} - \frac{\sum_i n_i}{T}\frac{dT}{dz} \qquad 3.8$$

The general law governing the distribution of a given constituent with height in a static atmosphere is then:

$$\frac{1}{n_i}\frac{dn_i}{dz} = -\frac{m_i g}{kT} - \frac{1}{T}\frac{dT}{dz} \qquad 3.9$$

Integration of Eq. 3.9 to find the number concentration of a given constituent, n_i, as a function of height gives:

$$n_i(z) = \frac{n_i(z_o)T(z_o)}{T(z)} \exp[-\int_{z_o}^{z} \frac{m_i g(z)}{kT(z)} dz] \qquad 3.10$$

where z_o is some reference height, usually taken as the height at which diffusive equilibrium begins.

The variation of the gravitational acceleration with height is given by:

$$g(z) = g_o \left[\frac{R_o}{R_o+Z}\right]^2 \qquad \textbf{3.11}$$

where g_o is the value of the gravitational acceleration at the surface, which is at a distance R_o from the center of the earth. The number concentration of a given constituent, n_i, then depends on the local temperature $T(z)$, the temperature at the reference height $T(z_o)$, and on an integral involving the temperature distribution between z_o and z. The distribution of temperature thus enters critically in the variation in number concentration of a given constituent. The reference height is usually taken to be equal to the height at which diffusive separation occurs and below which convective mixing prevails. A problem of importance is the determination of this level and a description of the gradation between convection and diffusion. In general, the concentration and temperature at the reference level will vary with time.

It is helpful to define a variable $H(z)$, called the scale height by:

$$H(z) = \frac{kT(z)}{m_i g(z)} \qquad \textbf{3.12}$$

This variable is the equivalent depth of an atmosphere as if it were incompressible. The density of such an atmosphere is constant throughout its depth. This is only a hypothetical construct but is a useful mathematical tool. To visualize the source of this relationship, consider the simple situation where a single constituent forms a homogeneous atmosphere and the acceleration due to gravity is constant. If we assume this atmosphere has a constant density with height, we can divide it into layers of equal geometric thickness. Each layer will have the same weight per unit area, so that each layer will contribute equally to the total pressure at the bottom. Since the surface pressure cannot be infinite, there must be only a finite number of layers. That is, the homogeneous atmosphere has only a finite total height which we will call H, the height of the homogeneous atmosphere or scale height.

If we integrate Eq. 3.1 from the surface, where the pressure is P_o, to height H, where the pressure is zero, we get:

$$\int_{P_o}^{P=0} dP = -\rho g \int_{H=0}^{H} dz \qquad \textbf{3.13}$$

or

$$P_o = \rho g H \qquad \textbf{3.14}$$

Now, substituting Eqs. 3.2 and 3.3 into Eq. 3.14 for a single constituent atmosphere:

$$n_o k T_o = m_i n_o g H \qquad \textbf{3.15}$$

and solving for H:

$$H = \frac{kT_o}{m_i g} \qquad \textbf{3.16}$$

This simple case results in a definition for the scale height similar in form to Eq. 3.14. The height of a homogeneous atmosphere is a function only of the temperature at the surface and known constants. For dry air on earth with T_o = 273 K, H ≅ 8 km. Eq. 3.12 has a similar meaning, except that the gravitational acceleration is allowed to vary.

If the scale height from Eq. 3.12 is now substituted into Eq. 3.10 the following simplified relation is found:

$$n_i(z) = \frac{n_i(z_o)T(z_o)}{T(z)} \exp[-\frac{(z-z_o)}{H(z_o)}] \qquad \textbf{3.17}$$

For an isothermal atmosphere, $T(z_o) = T(z)$ so:

$$n_i(z) = n_i(z_o)\exp[-\frac{(z-z_o)}{H(z_o)}] \qquad \textbf{3.18}$$

The number concentration decreases exponentially with height. As a result, there is no upper boundary to this atmosphere; it thins out gradually with elevation and the number concentration goes to zero only at $z = \infty$. The height of the corresponding homogeneous atmosphere appears as a parameter. When $z-z_o = H$, the number concentration will be $1/e$ of its value at z_o.

We now have a relationship in Eq. 3.18 for the number concentration of gas molecules as a function of height and temperature distribution. Because of their thermal energy, the gas molecules are in motion and have a velocity distribution determined by the temperature. We have yet to determine the rate at which particles at any given level may escape. The two necessary conditions for escape to take place are that the vertical velocity of an outgoing particle is greater than the critical escape velocity, v_e, and that the particle with this velocity has a negligible chance of undergoing a collision which returns it to the lower atmosphere. The escape velocity is defined by the requirement that the particle's kinetic energy is greater than the gravitational potential energy. If we say that they are equal:

$$\tfrac{1}{2}mv_e^2(z) = mg(z)(R_o + z) \qquad \textbf{3.19}$$

where m is the mass of the particle, $g(z)$ is the gravitational acceleration at an arbitrary height z above the surface of the earth, and R_o is the radius of the earth. Solving Eq. 3.19 for v_e results in:

$$v_e = \sqrt{2g(z)(R_o + Z)} \qquad \textbf{3.20}$$

which can also be written as:

$$v_e = \sqrt{\frac{2GM}{(R_o+z)}} \quad \textbf{3.21}$$

since:

$$g(z) = \frac{GM}{(R_o+z)^2} \quad \textbf{3.22}$$

where G is the gravitational constant (6.673×10^{-11} Nm^2/kg^2) and M is the mass of the earth.

The critical escape velocity is independent of the mass of the particle but dependent on the gravitational acceleration of the planet and the distance from the surface or, as expressed in Eq. 3.21, dependent on the gravitational constant, the mass of the planet, and the distance from the surface. Fig. 3.1 shows the escape velocity as a function of distance above the earth's surface.

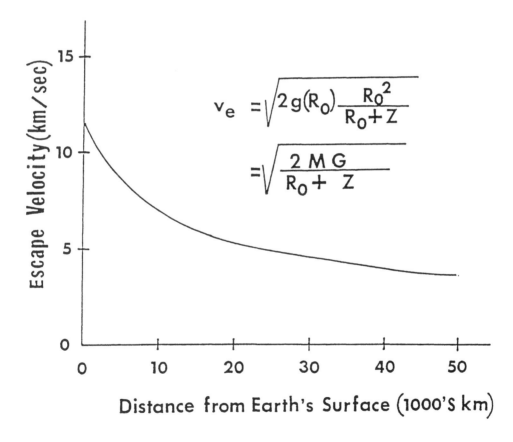

Figure 3.1 Escape speed *vs.* distance from the surface of the earth, where g is the acceleration due to gravity, R_o is the radius of the earth, z is the height above the earth's surface, and M is the mass of the earth.

Now, imagine a relatively large container filled with n molecules of a certain gas at a relatively low pressure. The available energy will be distributed over the n molecules in such a way that there are many more molecules with small velocities than with large velocities. The component of velocities in one direction, say the x direction, will give a distribution of v_x as shown in Fig. 3.2.

This normal or Gaussian distribution has the mathematical form:

$$f(v_x) = A_x e^{-bv_x^2} \qquad 3.23$$

where A_x is the concentration of particles per unit velocity which has zero velocity and b is a coefficient which determines the broadness of the velocity distribution.

The number of molecules per unit volume which have velocities between v_x and $v_x + dv_x$ describes the Maxwell velocity distribution:

$$f(v_x)dv_x = A_x e^{-bv_x^2} dv_x \qquad 3.24$$

Generalizing this result to three dimensions gives:

$$f(v)dv = A e^{-b(v_x^2+v_y^2+v_z^2)} dv_x dv_y dv_z \qquad 3.25$$

The speed v of a molecule is just $(v_x^2 + v_y^2 + v_z^2)^{1/2}$, and we wish to know the distribution of speeds $f(v)dv$. In order to find this distribution, we must know how dv is related to dv_x, dv_y, and dv_z as shown in Fig. 3.3.

The points of constant v form the surface of a spherical shell of thickness dv. The volume of the spherical shell is $4\pi v^2 dv$. Replacing the "volume" element $dv_x dv_y dv_z$ with $4\pi v^2 dv$ in Eq. 3.25, we obtain the Maxwell speed distribution:

$$f(v)dv = 4\pi A e^{-bv^2} v^2 dv \qquad 3.26$$

This function is plotted in Fig. 3.4. To find the constants in Eq. 3.26, two conditions must be satisfied. The constant A is the normalization constant and is chosen so that the integral over all speeds gives the total number of molecules (per unit volume) in the container of gas:

$$\int_0^\infty f(v)dv = N \qquad 3.27$$

We also know from kinetic theory that the average kinetic energy per molecule of a gas in thermal equilibrium is 3/2kT, or:

$$\frac{1}{N}\int_0^\infty (\tfrac{1}{2}mv^2)f(v)dv = \tfrac{3}{2}kT \qquad 3.28$$

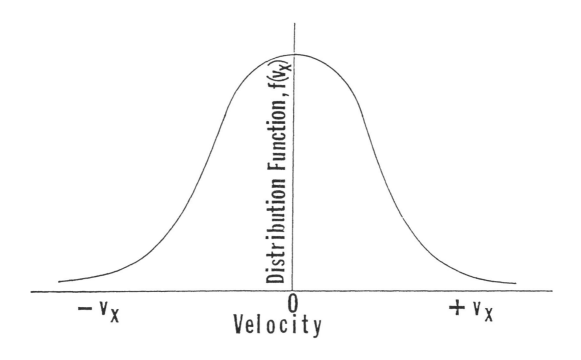

Figure 3.2   Gaussian speed distribution function.

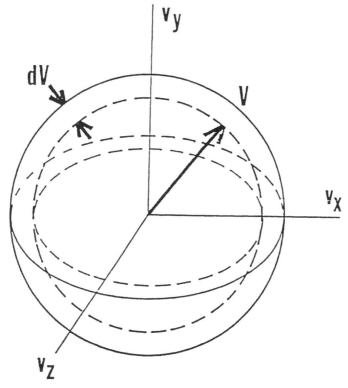

Figure 3.3   Three-dimensional velocity space relating the change in dv to dv_x, dv_y, and dv_z.

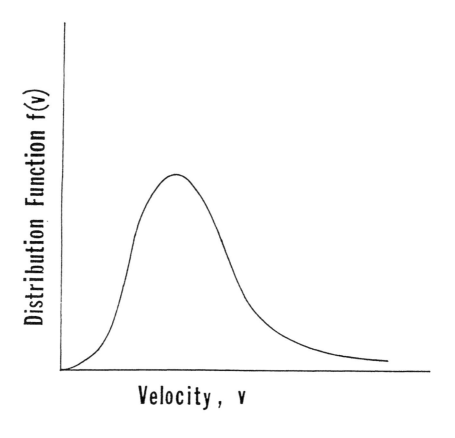

Figure 3.4   Maxwellian speed distribution function.

Solving Eqs. 3.27 and 3.28 simultaneously, results in:

$$A = N(\tfrac{m}{2\pi kT})^{\tfrac{3}{2}} \qquad \textbf{3.29}$$

and

$$b = \tfrac{m}{2kT} \qquad \textbf{3.30}$$

so that:

$$f(v)dv = 4\pi N v^2 (\tfrac{m}{2\pi kT})^{\tfrac{3}{2}} \exp^{-\tfrac{mv^2}{2kT}} dv \qquad \textbf{3.31}$$

where N is the number density of the constituent in question and T is the absolute temperature.

Eq. 3.31 now gives us the concentration of particles over a small velocity interval, dv. This distribution of velocities is isotropic, *i.e.*, the number of particles traveling in all directions is the same. However, we are interested in the concentration of particles traveling outward from the earth. We must develop a factor by which Eq. 3.31 can be multiplied to calculate the concentration as a function of direction. Fig. 3.5 shows the geometry of particle motion relative to a vertical axis through the center of the earth.

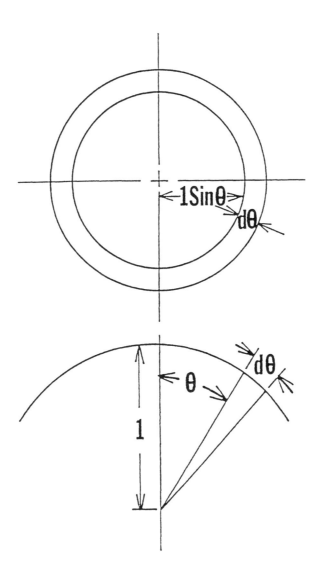

Figure 3.5　　Geometry relating the upward vertical component of velocity to the sphere of all possible velocities.

The factor we desire is the ratio of the area of a ring of width, dθ, encircling the vertical axis to the total area of a sphere of unit radius through which the particles can travel.

$$Factor = \frac{Area\_of\_Ring}{Total\_Area\_of\_Sphere} \qquad 3.32$$

Now, the area of the ring is the circumference of the ring, $2\pi r$ times the width of the ring, $d\theta$. However, r is $(1)\sin\theta$, so that:

$$Area\_of\_Ring = 2\pi(1)\sin\theta d\theta \qquad 3.33$$

where the total area of the sphere is $4\pi(1)^2$, so that:

$$Factor = \frac{2\pi(1)\sin\theta d\theta}{4\pi(1)^2} = \frac{\sin\theta d\theta}{2} \qquad 3.34$$

The concentration of particles over a velocity interval, dv, and moving with a velocity vector between θ and $d\theta$, is then:

$$f(v)dv[\tfrac{\sin\theta d\theta}{2}] \qquad 3.35$$

The vertical flux is this concentration multiplied by the vertical component of the velocity, $v\cos\theta$:

$$f(v)dv[\tfrac{\sin\theta d\theta}{2}]v\cos\theta \qquad 3.36$$

The total upward vertical flux is obtained by integrating over the upper hemisphere centered on the vertical axis. The total vertical flux of particles is then:

$$\int_0^{\frac{\pi}{2}} f(v)dv \frac{v\cos\theta \sin\theta}{2} d\theta = \tfrac{1}{4}vf(v)dv \qquad 3.37$$

To find the escape flux at the base of the exosphere, this expression is integrated over all velocities greater than the escape velocity:

$$F_e = \int_{v_e}^{\infty} N_e \tfrac{1}{4} v 4\pi v^2 (\tfrac{m}{2\pi kT})^{\frac{3}{2}} \exp[-\tfrac{mv^2}{2kT(z)}] dv \qquad 3.38$$

or:

$$F_e = N_e \pi (\tfrac{m}{2\pi kT})^{\frac{3}{2}} \int_{v_e}^{\infty} v^3 \exp[-\tfrac{mv^2}{2kT}] dv \qquad 3.39$$

where N_e is the particle number density at the base of the exosphere.

When Eq. 3.39 is integrated, it becomes:

$$F_e = N_e \pi \left(\frac{m}{2\pi kT}\right)^{\frac{3}{2}} \left(\frac{kT}{m}\right) [v_e^2 + \frac{2kT}{m}] \exp[-\frac{mv_e^2}{2kT}] \qquad \textbf{3.40}$$

Substituting from Eq. 3.20 for v_e:

$$F_e = N_e [\frac{kT}{2\pi m}]^{\frac{1}{2}} [1 + \frac{mg(z_e)}{kT}(R_o + z_e)] \exp[-\frac{mg(z_e)}{kT}(R_o + z_e)] \qquad \textbf{3.41}$$

Substituting from Eq. 3.12 for $mg(z_e)/kT$:

$$F_e = N_e [\frac{g(z_e)H_e}{2\pi}]^{\frac{1}{2}} [1 + \frac{R_o + z_e}{H_e}] \exp[-\frac{(R_o + z_e)}{H_e}] \qquad \textbf{3.42}$$

where H_e is the scale height at the base of the exosphere, called the exobase and z_e is the height of the exobase above the surface of the earth. Note, that the units have come out correctly. If N_e is in units of molecules/m^3, then F_e will be in units of molecules/m^2/sec. In order to evaluate the escape flux, we must locate the exobase. The concept of a sharp transition between the region of the atmosphere dominated by collisions and an overlying collisionless region is an idealization of a gradual transition, so the location of the exobase is to some degree arbitrary. If there are no further collisions at heights greater than z_e, F_e equals the escape loss; otherwise it is just the outward flux. The physical interpretation of Eq. 3.42 thus depends critically on the relative frequency of collisions beyond a given level.

The conditions for the validity of Eq. 3.42 have been discussed in great detail by Opik and Singer (1959), Opik (1960), Brandt and Chamberlain (1960), Herring and Kyle (1961), and Aamondt and Case (1962). Within the region of the atmosphere where collisions are frequent, the Maxwellian distribution on which Eq. 4.42 is based holds quite accurately, and gives a direct estimate of the outward flux. However, part of this outward flux is balanced by an inward flux due to the fact that a certain fraction of the particles in their upward paths collide and return. The net outward flux is then less than that given by Eq. 4.42. As the base of the exosphere is approached, the total net flux is more closely approximated by Eq. 4.42, but because of the absence of collisions, the Maxwellian distribution holds less exactly. Because of this difficulty, Fahr and Shizgal (1983) have stated that a rigorous description of the velocity distribution function for all altitudes including the transition region near the base of the exosphere has not been achieved to date. They suggest that a kinetic theory description which takes into account both the change from collision-dominated to collisionless conditions and the effects due to the loss of particles to space needs to be constructed. Considerable effort has gone into estimating the difference from Jean's escape caused by non-Maxwellian conditions. Fahr and Shizgal (1983) imply that the rate of actual thermal escape is probably 70 - 80% of Jean's escape, although some calculations have been made that indicate the actual flux to be as little as 10-20% of the rate of Jean's escape. Certainly with these diverse estimates more work needs to be done before any great confidence can be placed in the thermal flux estimates. In any case, Jean's escape is likely to be an upper limit to the thermal flux.

Escape occurs from an isothermal region of the atmosphere at a level sufficiently high that all of the atmospheric gases normally have density profiles governed by diffusive equilibrium. Under these conditions, the density of each constituent varies approximately exponentially with altitude, at a rate determined by the mass of the constituent and not by the other gases present. To evaluate Eq. 3.42, we find the reference density N_e to be 3.4×10^{13} atoms/cm^3 at a height of about 100 km. The temperature at the homopause is approximately 185 K and the exospheric temperature averages about 1500 K. The concentration is further adjusted by the helium mixing ratio shown in Table 3.1. With these assumptions, the value of the helium flux is calculated to be 5×10^4 atoms/cm^2/sec. This escape rate is about 40 times less than the average source rate estimated to be coming into the atmosphere from the crust of the earth. By dividing this escape flux into the column density of helium in the atmosphere (1.1×10^{20} atoms/cm^2), the characteristic escape time for atmospheric helium is found to be about 70 million years. Column density is defined as the number of atoms through the depth of the atmosphere above an area of 1 cm^2 at the earth's surface. By dividing the source flux of 2×10^6 atoms/cm^2/sec into the column density, the residence time is found to be about 2 million years. Thus, the characteristic residence time for helium is much smaller than the characteristic escape time. In other words, it takes a much longer time for a given quantity of helium to escape from the atmosphere to space than it does to enter the atmosphere from the crust.

Since the old-earth modelers are convinced that the earth is 4.5 billion years old, Walker (1977) then states, "...there appears to be a problem with the helium budget of the atmosphere." MacDonald (1964) has evaluated the escape flux averaged over an entire 11-year cycle of solar activity, using satellite data to evaluate exospheric temperature. He found an average escape flux of 6×10^4 atoms/cm^2/sec, a factor of 30 less than the source. Spitzer (1949) and Hunten (1973) have suggested that the bulk of the escape occurs during infrequent periods of high temperature. They suggest that if the exospheric temperature were to be raised to 2000 K by solar flares or cosmic bombardment of some type, diffusion of the helium up through the lower atmosphere would become the limiting process and the escape flux would be equal to 1×10^8 atoms/cm^2/sec. Walker (1977) suggests that if hot episodes occurred only 2% of the time an average loss rate of 2×10^6 atoms/cm^2/sec could be attained. The helium would accumulate slowly between the hot episodes and escape rapidly during them. He suggests that, perhaps, we have not observed such a hot episode in recent history.

Non-thermal Escape of Helium

If one is convinced that the age of the earth is 4.5 billion years and the present amount of helium in the atmosphere would accumulate in about 2 million years, then there must be some other loss process in addition to thermal escape. Three of the more popular suggestions are 1) polar wind, 2) solar wind sweeping, and 3) hot-ion exchange.

Mechanisms other than thermal escape are considered even by the old-earth scientific community to be speculative and of undetermined significance. It should be recognized that more loss mechanisms will likely be proposed in the future, in the hope that this dilemma will one day be resolved without resorting to a re-examination of the age of the earth's atmosphere.

The polar wind is the escape of light ions such as H^+ and H_e^+ through open magnetic field lines near the poles of the earth. The well-developed magnetosphere on earth has magnetic lines of force originating near or at the poles which are not closed onto the planet, but open out into the interplanetary medium. The field lines originating at latitudes greater than 75° are open, corresponding to about 1/40 of the earth's surface. Ions and electrons are accelerated along these open field lines and escape the earth's atmosphere at polar latitudes. A polar breeze model developed by Banks and Holzer (1969) argues that collisions are unimportant and exhibits features similar to Jean's escape. Both are limited by thermal diffusion from the lower atmosphere and to the polar regions. Axford (1968) has applied the polar wind model specifically to the escape of helium and calculated an escape flux of about 1×10^5 atoms/cm^2/sec, much lower than even Jean's escape.

Solar wind sweeping is a process by which the solar wind plasma, made up mainly of protons and electrons flowing outward from the sun at high velocities, interacts with the magnetosphere of a planet, deforming it and sweeping particles away into space. If the planet has a strong magnetic field like earth's, the effects will be minimal. The solar wind particles become thermalized at a bow shock which typically lies several planetary radii from the surface. The thermalized particles flow into the magnetosheath which lies between the bow shock and the magnetopause and are swept around the planet. They do not, in general, penetrate the magnetopause, and thus have a negligible effect on the atmosphere which lies below. Michel (1971) and Cloutier, *et al.* (1969) have developed methods for estimating the loss rates due to the solar wind which, in general, are quite low for the earth.

Hot-ion exchange is a process whereby an energetic ion transfers its kinetic energy to a neutral particle like helium, which can then escape. Hot-ion exchange is discussed by Fahr and Shizgal (1983) for hydrogen escape from Earth, Venus, and Mars, but little has been done on the escape of helium from Earth. The escape rates by hot-ion exchange seem to be low, but some researchers believe this process has the best potential for explaining the loss of helium.

Conclusions and Recommendations

The flux of ^{4}He from the crust of the earth into the atmosphere is estimated to be about 2×10^6 atoms/cm^2/sec. The flux from the atmosphere to space by thermal escape is estimated to be 5×10^4 atoms/cm^2/sec. Other escape mechanisms such as the polar wind, solar wind sweeping, and hot-ion exchange have not been found to be important contributors to the loss of helium. If the earth's atmosphere had no helium when it was formed, the current measured column density of helium (1.1×10^{20} atoms/cm^2) would have been produced in about 2 million years. This is over 2000 times shorter than the presumed age of the earth. Old-earth atmospheric physicists such as Walker (1977) state that, "...there appears to be a problem with the helium budget of the atmosphere." Chamberlain and Hunten (1987) states that this helium escape problem, "...will not go away, and it is unsolved."

I believe the source of this problem is the assumption that the earth's atmosphere is billions of years old. An alternative model is that the atmosphere is relatively young (less than 10,000 years) and that the helium content of the atmosphere is mostly primordial or was produced in a recent burst of radioactive activity at Creation, in the Judgment in the Garden of Eden, or during the Flood. During the 10,000 years or so since the Creation, less than 1% of today's helium would have been added to the atmosphere by the decay of radioactive materials in the crust under rates observed today.

Obviously, more work needs to be done on this subject. The study of the influx and outflux processes of gases like hydrogen, helium, argon, neon, and krypton may lead to better estimates of the age of the earth's atmosphere. Investigation of the sources of the heavier gases may be particularly illuminating, since uncertainties by thermal escape can be eliminated from consideration. I recommend that the sources of argon, neon, and krypton especially be investigated and their residence times calculated. In all such studies of this nature, care should be taken not to incorporate old-earth assumptions into observations and calculations.

CHAPTER 4

ICE CORE ANALYSES

In the late 1980's and early 1990's my interest in paleoclimate began to broaden to consider a young-earth explanation for the formation of polar ice sheets and mountain glaciers during the "ice age." A new ice core was being drilled at Summit, Greenland and frequent statements were being released in the scientific and popular literature that ice at the bottom of the Greenland ice sheet was 250,000 or more years old. Since the Bible clearly teaches that the earth is less than 10,000 years old, how is it possible for ice in Greenland to be dated at 250,000 years? Was there a young-earth explanation?

Although I was not trained in glaciology, and my background was in cloud physics, precipitation physics, and meteorology, this subject seemed like a natural extension of my training and experience. A new Federal law had just been adopted which made it possible for me to obtain data which had been collected and computer programs which had been developed under government funding. This included ice core data and global climate models. Since ICR would not likely ever be able to afford to fund field work and model development which cost millions of dollars, I saw this as a magnificent opportunity for creationists to make major contributions in a new field. Sometime around 1994 I expected the original data from the ice core at Summit, Greenland to be available for analysis. Due to the reluctance of some of the principal investigators to release the data and problems with archiving the data, it was not actually available until 1996. However, this didn't prevent me from beginning to develop conceptual models and preliminary numerical models of how the ice and snow accumulated in the polar regions.

Four other events occurred in the early 1990's which made it possible for ICR to begin a major thrust into paleoclimatology. First, Mike Oard submitted a draft manuscript to ICR which became a monograph entitled, *An Ice Age Caused by the Genesis Flood.* Oard (1990) suggested a new concept that energy released during the Genesis Flood into the oceans caused increased evaporation which, in turn, produced heavy snow in the polar regions and on mountains leading to the "ice age." Cooling of the oceans following the Flood lead to reduced snowfall and eventually, the end of the "ice age". This basic mechanism for an explanation of the "ice age" following the Genesis Flood has formed the basis for much of my work since then.

Second, the continued development of PCs with higher-speed CPUs, greater memory, and FORTRAN compilers permitted numerical modeling and data analysis to be done on a scale that was competitive with work which had only been done before on mainframe computers. Steve Low and his associates at Hewlett Packard in Roseville, California donated several PCs and peripherals to the effort during the early 1990s which made this whole effort possible.

Third, I was able to obtain a copy of CCM1, a global climate model developed at the National Center for Atmospheric Research (NCAR). Although I was provided the FORTRAN program, i41t was designed to run on a CRAY computer. A CRAY was the state-of-the-art supercomputer in 1990. No help was forthcoming from NCAR to adapt it to run on a PC. Not only does a CRAY run much faster than a PC, it also has much more memory, allowing the program to call more numerous and larger arrays and store more output. I needed help to modify the program.

The fourth event which allowed ICR to begin serious research in paleoclimatology was an offer by Herman Daily, a government programmer at the China Lake Naval Weapons Center, to offer his programming services free of charge once he retired the following year. Good to his word upon retirement, Herman began adapting the CCM1 program to run on one of the PCs donated to ICR. By 1992 we were beginning to obtain meaningful output from CCM1.

A Young-earth Age Model for Ice Cores

During the time it took to put the programming together with the hardware, software, and data to do climate modeling, I spent most of my time for the next few years developing conceptual and numerical models of the accumulation of snow in the polar regions. I acquired ice core data from the National Geophysical Data Center (NGDC) in Boulder, Colorado for Camp Century, Milcent, Crete, and Dye in Greenland and Vostok, Byrd, Siple, and Dome C in Antarctica. The main variables measured in these cores were $\delta^{18}O$, CO_2, CH_4, dust, and electrical conductivity.

The most important variable is $\delta^{18}O$ because of its relationship to environmental temperature. It is a measure of the difference in the ratio of oxygen isotopes in a sample of ice compared to that in a sample of ocean water today. The definition is:

$$\delta^{18}O = \frac{(^{18}O/^{16}O) - (^{18}O/^{16}O)_{SMOW}}{(^{18}O/^{16}O)_{SMOW}} * 1000‰ \qquad (4.1)$$

where $(^{18}O/^{16}O)$ is the ratio of the masses of the oxygen-18 to oxygen-16 isotopes in a sample, and $(^{18}O/^{16}O)_{SMOW}$ is this ratio in a sample of Standard Mean Ocean Water (SMOW) today. The ratio is multiplied by 1000 to express its magnitude in mils (‰, parts/thousand).

$\delta^{18}O$ is related to temperature because of the difference in evaporation and sublimation rates for water molecules which contain ^{18}O or ^{16}O atoms. Air is left enriched in water molecules with ^{16}O atoms after either an evaporation or sublimation process relative to ^{18}O atoms because the heavier ^{18}O atoms tend to stay in the denser liquid state. The warmer the temperature, the greater the effect. Consequently, $\delta^{18}O$ can be used as a paleothermometer. One conversion equation is given by (Johnsen *et al.*, 1989):

$$\delta^{18}O = 0.667T - 13.7‰ \qquad (4.2)$$

Fig. 4.1 shows $\delta^{18}O$ as a function of depth at Camp Century. Note, that most of the variation in $\delta^{18}O$ occurs near the bottom of the core. These changes are believed to be caused by the latest ice age according to conventional interpreters. The upper portion of the core has a uniform value of about -30‰ at about -20°C. At the bottom of the core $\delta^{18}O$ is more negative with temperatures estimated to be colder than -40°C.

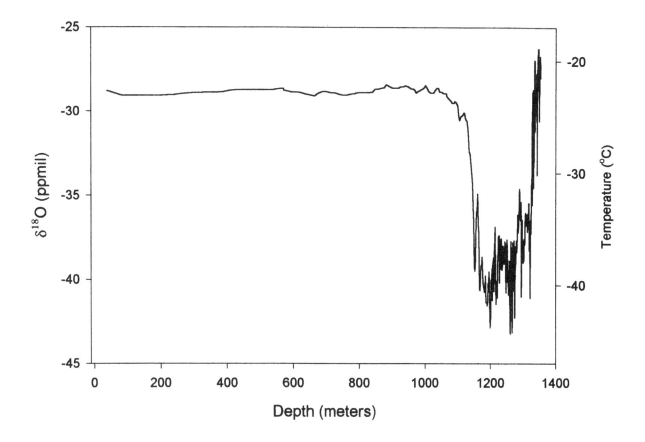

Figure 4.1 $\delta^{18}O$ vs. depth for Camp Century, Greenland.

We wish to develop a young-earth age scale which is consistent with a Biblical chronology. Development of the following young-earth model may be found in Vardiman (1993), *"Ice Cores and the Age of the Earth,"* and Vardiman (1994) following Nye (1951, 1957, 1959). Fig. 4.2 shows a schematic of ice flowing outward and downward near an ice divide. An ice divide is a topographic feature from which the ice diverges. The layers of ice compress as they move downward and get thinner due to the weight of the overlying ice and snow. Fig. 4.3 shows the time and height variables of a layer in an ice sheet at a distance, x, from an ice divide. Nye assumed an infinite sheet of ice of uniform thickness of H meters, which accumulates snow everywhere on its upper surface at a rate of λ_H/τ meters/year. Thinning of the ice sheet is restricted to the y direction and horizontal flow to the x direction only. This model implies sliding on the bottom.

For an ice sheet in mass balance (the accumulation rate from precipitation equals the ablation rate by compression and spreading) the continuity equation is:

$$\frac{\lambda_H}{\tau}x = V_x H \qquad (4.3)$$

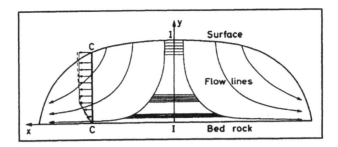

Figure 4.2 Flow model of ice flowing outward from an ice divide (Dansgaard, et al., 1971).

where τ is the accumulation period in years (typically one year), λ_H is the accumulation over the accumulation period in meters of ice, x is the horizontal distance from the ice divide along the flow direction, V_x is the velocity in the x direction, and H is the thickness of the ice sheet in meters.

If the ice is assumed to be incompressible, then the divergence of the velocity is zero, or:

$$\nabla \bullet V = 0 \tag{4.4}$$

where $V = \mathbf{i}V_x + \mathbf{j}V_y$, is the total velocity vector.

Eq. 4.4 becomes:

$$\frac{\partial V_x}{\partial x} + \frac{\partial V_y}{\partial y} = 0 \tag{4.5}$$

where y is the distance from the bottom of the ice sheet and V_y is the velocity, positive in the upward direction. Since it will be assumed that no motion or divergence occurs in the third direction, z, it is sufficient to consider the problem in two dimensions only.

We wish to find a relation between the height in a column of ice, y, and Δt, the elapsed time since ice at that depth fell as fresh snow. From Eq. 4.3:

$$\frac{\partial V_x}{\partial x} = \frac{\lambda_H}{H\tau} \tag{4.6}$$

Combining Eqs. 4.5 and 4.6:

$$\frac{\partial V_x}{\partial x} = -\frac{\partial V_y}{\partial y} = \frac{\lambda_H}{H\tau} \tag{4.7}$$

Integrating and solving for V_y:

$$\int_0^{V_y} dV_y = -\frac{\lambda_H}{H\tau} \int_o^y dy \tag{4.8}$$

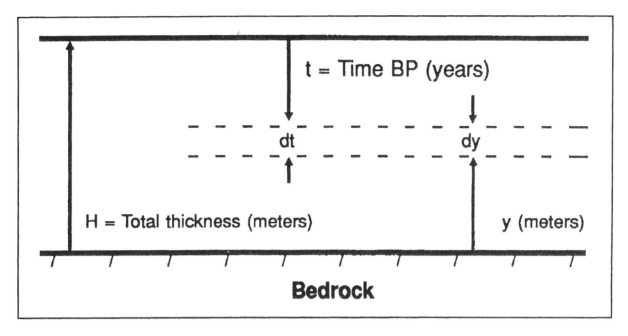

Figure 4.3   Schematic of time and height variables of a layer in an ice sheet at a distance, *x*, from the ice divide.

or:

$$V_y = -\frac{\lambda_H}{H\tau}y \tag{4.9}$$

The time in the past when a given layer was laid down can then, theoretically, be calculated by solving for the time interval Δt:

$$V_y = \frac{dy}{dt} \tag{4.10}$$

or:

$$dt = \frac{dy}{V_y} \tag{4.11}$$

Integrating downward from the surface in the -*y* direction corresponds to an integration backward in time. At the surface *y = H* and *t = 0*, so:

$$\int_0^{\Delta t} dt = \int_H^y \frac{dy}{V_y} \tag{4.12}$$

or, from Eq. 4.5:

$$\Delta t = -\frac{H\tau}{\lambda_H} \int_H^y \frac{dy}{y} = \frac{H\tau}{\lambda_H} \ln\frac{H}{y} \tag{4.13}$$

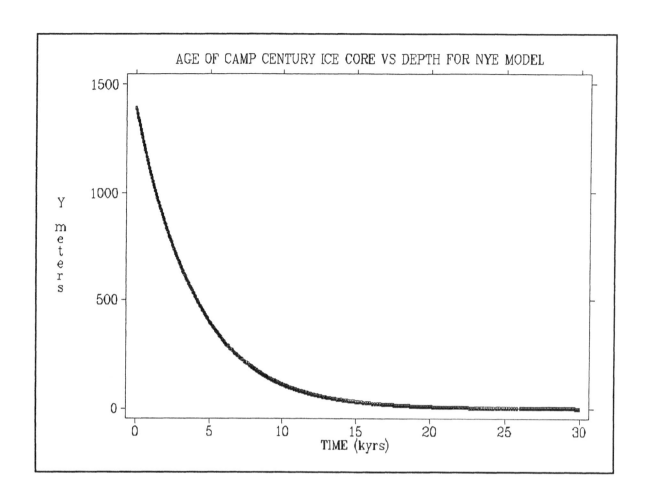

Figure 4.4   Nye model age *vs.* height above base for Camp Century.

Upon applying this old-earth age model to the Camp Century data, the variation of $\delta^{18}O$ with height above the base of the ice sheet appears as shown in Fig. 4.4 and $\delta^{18}O$ with conventional time in Fig. 4.5. Note, that with this age model the data in the lower part of the core has been expanded dramatically and the upper part compressed compared to Fig. 4.1. The coldest part of the core is estimated to occur about 18,000 years ago, according to conventional dating, following a gradual decrease in temperature. At about 18,000 years ago the temperature increased suddenly during the deglaciation to the Holocene period where it becomes uniform with time. This flat section of the graph is interpreted to be interglacial.

My challenge was to develop a young-earth creationist age scale for these same data and interpret the results. The old-earth model assumes that the ice sheets in Greenland and Antarctica have been around for millions of years and are in equilibrium. That is, the precipitation rate has been uniform for millions of years and the ice sheet compresses and spreads horizontally at the same rate as the precipitation is added to the top. It is this uniformitarian assumption which gives rise to the very great ages for the bottom ice (infinite age at the very bottom) which these models yield. A young-earth model, on the other hand, assumes that the ice sheet has only been in

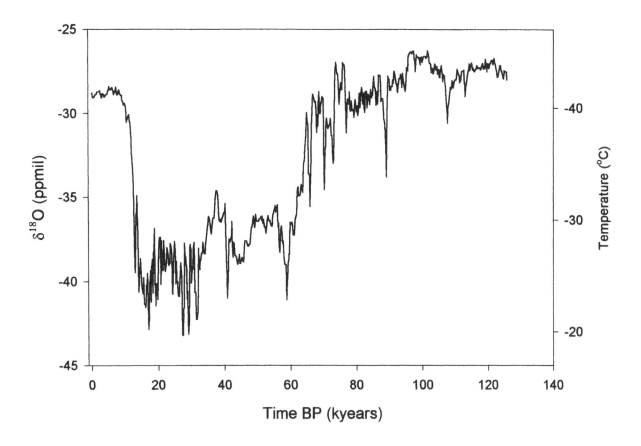

Figure 4.5 $\delta^{18}O$ *vs.* conventional time for Camp Century, Greenland.

existence since the Genesis Flood about 4,500 years ago and that the ice sheet is probably not in equilibrium, but may be compressing and spreading at a different rate than the precipitation which is being added to the top would imply. In addition, the precipitation rate has probably changed in the past, although it may be uniform now.

Assume that a sheet of ice of thickness, H, accumulates snow on its upper surface at a rate of λ/τ meters/year, where λ is the accumulation in meters over a time period, τ, in years. In this case, we will *not* assume that the ice sheet is in mass balance, but, rather, that it grows rapidly following the Flood, and later approaches the equilibrium condition observed today. This means that H is a function of time, rather than being constant as the uniformitarian model requires. In fact, H will be assumed to be 0 at $t = 0$, the end of the Flood. The thickness of the ice sheet is then a function of the accumulation rate and the rate of thinning. The conventional old-earth model developed a flow regime based on a two-dimensional assumption of incompressibility (Eq. 4.4). However, in this young-earth model, I will use a linear thinning function which is calibrated by the observed compression. In other words, the compression of an ice layer will be proportional to the thickness of the ice sheet.

This simple model can then be expressed as:

$$\frac{dH}{dt} = \lambda/\tau - \delta H \qquad (4.14)$$

where H is the thickness of the ice sheet in meters as a function of time, t is the accumulation period in years, λ is the accumulation over the accumulation period in meters, and δ is the thinning ratio in year^{-1}. The thinning ratio is a constant and will be determined from the boundary conditions.

Eq. 4.14 says that the rate of change in the thickness of the ice sheet is the difference between the accumulation rate of snow, falling on the upper surface and the compression of the ice sheet which is linearly proportional to its thickness. This model assumes a linear thinning function, which may not always be the case, particularly when the stress and strain are outside the elastic limits. Non-linear thinning may occur when the ice is melting, during massive surging, or when the underlying terrain constrains horizontal motions.

Before we can solve Eq. 4.14, we need to assume a functional form for λ. We have reason to believe, from our Flood model, that immediately following the Flood the oceans were warm and the continents and polar regions were cold, compared to that of today (Oard, 1990). If this was the case, the precipitation rate likely would have been much greater than that of today, and would have decreased with time. We will assume an exponentially decreasing accumulation function, which approaches today's rate in the limit. We will further assume that the accumulation rate at the end of the Flood was some factor, Φ, times that of today. This factor will become a parameter which can be adjusted to obtain the best fit to observed data.

The functional form of λ described in the preceding paragraph then becomes:

$$\lambda = \lambda_H (\Phi e^{-\frac{t}{\Psi}} + 1) \qquad (4.15)$$

where λ_H is the accumulation over a period of time observed today, Φ is the factor of the precipitation rate at the end of the Flood multiplied by that of today, t is the time since the Flood, and Ψ is the e-folding time of the decrease in accumulation since the Flood. The e-folding time will be determined by the shape of the distribution of layers, to be explored shortly. Note, that when $t = 0$, in Eq. 4.15 $\lambda = (\Phi + 1)\lambda_H$ and when $t =$ infinity, $\lambda = \lambda_H$.

Combining Eqs. 4.14 and 4.15 and arranging into a standard form for the solution of a linear, time-dependent differential equation gives:

$$\frac{dH}{dt} + \delta H = \frac{\lambda_H}{\tau}(\Phi e^{-\frac{t}{\Psi}} + 1) \qquad (4.16)$$

The solution to this equation is:

$$H = \frac{\lambda_H}{\tau\delta}(1 - e^{-\delta t}) + \frac{\Phi \lambda_H}{\tau(\delta - \frac{1}{\Psi})}(e^{-\frac{t}{\Psi}} - e^{-\delta t}) \qquad (4.17)$$

Note, that Eq. 4.17 satisfies the boundary condition that $H = 0$ when $t = 0$. By applying another boundary condition, δ can be determined. Assume $H = 1370$ meters when $t =$ infinity. This is one of the boundary conditions for Camp Century. Under this condition, Eq. 4.17 reduces to:

$$H(t = \infty) = \frac{\lambda_H}{\tau\delta} = 1370 m \tag{4.18}$$

or:

$$\delta = \frac{\lambda_H}{(1370m)\tau} = 2.55 \times 10^{-4} year^{-1} \tag{4.19}$$

Fig. 4.6 shows the thickness of the Camp Century, Greenland ice sheet, H, plotted as a function of time since the Flood for a certain selection of parameters. In this case, $\lambda_H = .35$ m, $\tau = 1$, $\delta = 2.55 \times 10^{-4}$ year^{-1}, $\Psi = 400$ years, and the time since the Flood $t = 4,500$ years. Note that H starts at 0, increases rapidly, and asymptotically approaches today's thickness of 1370 meters. For smaller values of Ψ, the asymptotic approach to today's value is slower.

Fig. 4.6 illustrates the behavior of the entire thickness of the ice sheet, and deals primarily with the topmost layer. However, when ice cores are drilled down through the ice sheet today, we can measure the position of earlier layers which were formed and then buried. This additional information should help us develop a better estimate of the thinning function.

If we consider a given layer within the ice sheet, can we determine how far it has moved downward since it was formed? If we assume that the rate of movement downward of an ice layer is proportional to the thickness of the ice sheet and the position of a layer relative to the total thickness, we obtain:

$$V_y = \frac{dy}{dt} = -\delta \frac{y}{H_o} H(t) \tag{4.20}$$

where V_y is the vertical velocity of an ice layer relative to the base of the ice sheet, y is the position of a layer above the base, δ is the thinning ratio, H is the total thickness of the ice sheet as a function of time, and H_o is the total thickness today.

Now, at first, one might be tempted to define the downward velocity of a layer as proportional to the thickness of ice above the layer. However, it should be noted that the weight of the entire ice sheet is responsible for the movement of a given layer, because the rate at which the ice beneath a layer thins, allowing the layer to move downward, is dependent on the total thickness. Obviously, the preferable manner of deriving V_y would be to have a complete, time-dependent flow model showing the full two-dimensional movement of ice as a function of depth. This is not easily determined, so my model will assume a simple relationship for this first effort.

Eq. 4.20 says that the velocity of a layer is downward following its deposition and is proportional to the total thickness of the ice sheet. However, the factor, y/H_o, causes the

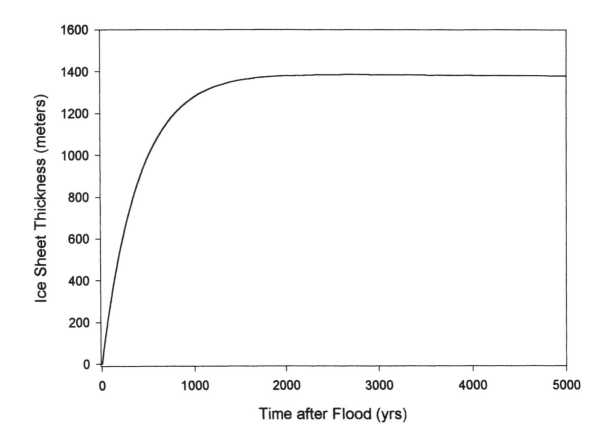

Figure 4.6 Thickness of the Camp Century ice sheet as a function of time after the Flood.

downward velocity to increase linearly from 0 at the bottom of the ice sheet to a maximum at the top. The bottom must be 0, because it rests on bedrock. The upper layers will subside faster, because of the accumulating compression.

Separating variables by transposing Eq. 4.20 results in:

$$\frac{dy}{y} = -\delta \frac{H(t)}{H_o} dt \qquad (4.21)$$

Substituting $H(t)$ from Eq. 4.17 and integrating to find the change in position, y, of an ice layer over the period of time since it was laid down, $\Delta t = t_{today} - t_{deposition}$ gives:

$$\int_{y_i}^{y} \frac{dy}{y} = -\int_0^{\Delta t} \frac{\delta}{H_o} [\frac{\lambda_H}{\tau \delta}(1 - e^{-\delta \tau}) + \frac{\Phi \lambda_H}{\tau(\delta - \frac{1}{\psi})}(e^{-\frac{t}{\psi}} - e^{-\delta \tau})] dt \qquad (4.22)$$

where y_i is the initial position of the layer when it was deposited and y is the position of the layer as a function of time after it was deposited.

Solving for y:

$$y = y_i e^{-\frac{\delta}{H_o}[\frac{\lambda_H}{\tau\delta}A + \frac{\Phi\lambda_H}{\tau(\delta-\frac{1}{\Psi})}B]} \quad (4.23)$$

where:

$$A = \Delta t + \frac{1}{\delta}(e^{-\delta\Delta t} - 1) \quad (4.24)$$

and:

$$B = -\frac{1}{\Psi}(e^{-\frac{\Delta t}{\Psi}} - 1) + \frac{1}{\delta}(e^{-\delta\Delta t} - 1) \quad (4.25)$$

Note, that Eq. 4.23 says that $y = y_i$ for $\Delta t = 0$. This means that the topmost layer, which is deposited today, 4,500 years after the Flood, has not yet begun to subside. Because the first layer at the end of the Flood was deposited at the position, $y_i = 0$, its position, y, will always be equal to *0*. Between the Flood and today, each layer will subside a varying amount, dependent upon the total thickness of the ice sheet, its position relative to the bottom of the sheet, and the length of time from its deposition until today.

Fig. 4.7 shows the position of the layers at Camp Century as a function of time since the Flood. The curve shows the greatest rate of change in layer position during the first 1,000 years after the Flood. This is due to the large change in snowfall rate immediately after the Flood. The decrease in accumulation was assumed to be exponential with a 400 year e-folding time. The top layer of the ice sheet will be precipitated at smaller increments above the preceding layers, and will be particularly noticeable immediately after the Flood. The curve is slightly concave upward during the last 3,000 years or so. This is due to the decreasing period of time available for the ice sheet to thin, as the top of the ice sheet is approached. At the very top, the most recent layer has not had time to thin at all, and its position is the same as the thickness of the ice sheet.

The curve in Fig. 4.7 can be used to estimate the age of the ice as a function of depth. Unfortunately, Eq. 4.23, which is the basis of Fig. 4.4, will not allow Δt, the period of time back to the formation of a layer, to be solved analytically. If one wishes to determine the age of a layer at a known depth, the age can be determined graphically from Fig. 4.7.

Now that we have a young-earth age model for the ice as a function of depth, it can be applied to the $\delta^{18}O$ data from Camp Century. The result is shown in Fig. 4.8. Note, that the curve of $\delta^{18}O$ versus the young-earth model time in Fig. 4.8 has the same general shape as the curve of $\delta^{18}O$ versus depth in Fig. 4.1. This is in major contrast to that of the old-earth model, which compresses the data near the top of the ice sheet and dramatically stretches the data near the bottom.

If the Flood occurred 4,500 years ago, as incorporated into this model, there would have been a quick "Ice Age" of about 500 years. $\delta^{18}O$ would have decreased from a high value at the end of the Flood to a minimum about 200-300 years later. The $\delta^{18}O$ would have then increased

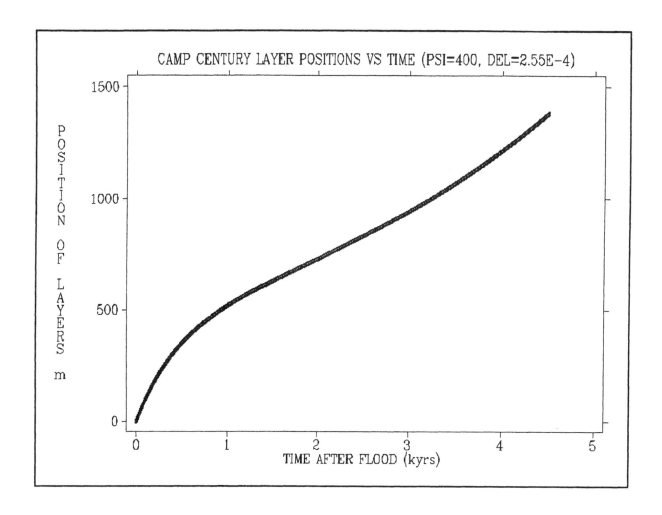

Figure 4.7   Position of ice layers at Camp Century as a function of time after the Flood.

rapidly from this minimum to the stable Holocene period in about 50 years. This latter change is in excellent agreement with the recent 4-year estimate by Alley et al. (1992, 1993) for the Younger Dryas transition.

Fig. 4.8 is the result of assuming a high precipitation rate following the Flood about 4,500 years ago which decreased exponentially to that of today. Several parameters were incorporated into this model, some of which were determined by boundary conditions. A list of the parameters in this young-earth creation model are shown in Table 4.1 with their definitions and the values used at Camp Century. It may be possible to derive an equally valid model with different parameters. It is important that further research be carried out to find the ranges over which these parameters are valid and, more importantly, if the model itself is valid. The way this can be done is to construct a similar relationship for other ice cores, particularly ones which have more precise data. The recent ice core from Summit, Greenland may have sufficient precision in the identification of layers to validate the model. For this reason, Jim Zavacky, a Masters student at ICR is attempting to compare model predictions and the observed number, thickness, and position of ice layers in the Summit core. It is already apparent from his research that some of the

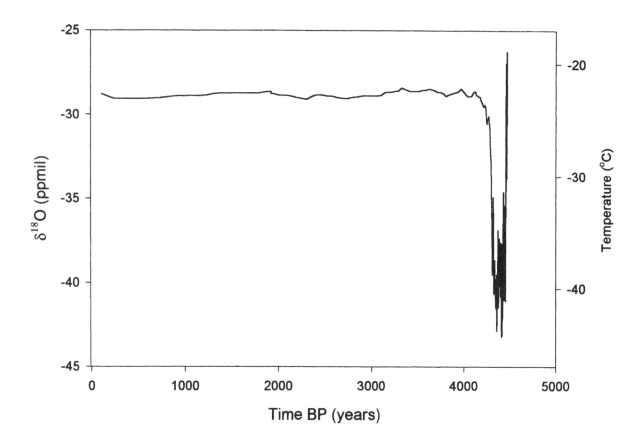

Figure 4.8 $\delta^{18}O$ vs. young-earth time for Camp Century, Greenland.

parameters will need to be adjusted. There is also evidence that more than one layer was probably formed each year deep in the core. The possibility was suggested by Vardiman (1993) that multiple layers may have been deposited yearly due to the chaotic nature of the weather immediately following the Flood. A mechanism for multiple layering, if it is confirmed, will need to be developed.

Another high quality ice core is currently being extracted from Antarctica. Data from this core could be available by 2002 or 2003. If it has precision measurements of layers similar to the Summit core, another study should be made on these data. The model could also be applied to the half dozen or so other cores which have been drilled to explore the range of model parameters.

Table 4.1 List of parameters in the young-earth ice sheet flow model.

Parameter	Definition	Value for Camp Century
H_o	Thickness of ice sheet today (m)	1,370
λ_H	Annual accumulation today (m)	0.35
Φ	Ratio of precipitation rate after Flood compared to today	10
Δt	Time since the Flood (years)	4,500
δ	Thinning ratio of ice sheet (year^{-1})	2.55×10^{-4}
Ψ	e-folding time of decrease in accumulation since the Flood (years)	400

The Conventional Explanation for the Variation of Oxygen Isotopes in Ice Cores

Correlation of paleotemperatures derived from ice cores and sea-floor sediments with variations in solar heating of the Earth caused by periodic changes in the orbital parameters of the Earth-Sun system has led to a widely-accepted explanation for the "Ice Ages" called the Astronomical Theory. This theory was originally suggested by Milankovitch (1930), but has recently gained popularity in such reports as CLIMAP (1976, 1981) and Hays *et al.* (1976).

Several major problems have not been resolved in this theory. First, of the three orbital parameters correlated in these studies the one with a period of about 100,000 years, which should be the cause of the "Ice Ages," has the smallest effect on solar heating of the Earth. It is so small that the "Ice Ages" can't be explained by its direct effects alone. This is the reason Hays *et al.* (1976) entitled their paper, "Variations in the Earth's orbit: *Pacemaker* of the Ice Ages." A secondary feedback mechanism in the ocean-atmosphere system is believed to be necessary.

Second, if such a secondary mechanism exists, it is not understood nor has it been quantified. This feedback mechanism, thought to be triggered by orbital variations, is the primary reason for current environmental extremism. It is believed that a minor perturbation in solar heating, caused by orbital changes, could lead to another "Ice Age" or warming period. If this is so, what changes in the climate would increased concentrations of greenhouse gases like carbon dioxide and ozone cause? We don't know the answer to this question. Our current state of knowledge about climate change is so poor that a suspicion that greenhouse may destabilize the climate does not justify the extreme environmental policy changes being considered today. Our poor understanding also does not support the Astronomical Theory.

Third, the orbital parameters should produce greater cooling or heating in the northern hemisphere than in the southern hemisphere historically. They should have lead to non-synchronous peaks in ice coverage in the two hemispheres. Yet, the "Ice Age" in the two hemispheres appears to have been synchronous.

Fourth, changes in the ice cover were recently found to have occurred at extremely high rates near the Younger Dryas Event. The Younger Dryas is a climate reversal preceded and followed by abrupt warming during the deglaciation period about 11,000 years BC, according to the conventional chronology. The event is documented in the $\delta^{18}O$ record of most ice cores and many sea-floor sediment cores. Alley *et al.* (1992, 1993) have reported that portions of the Younger Dryas appear to have occurred in periods of less than four years. If these processes occurred in such short periods, the entire chronology of the "Ice Age" is brought into question. For example, the average global ocean temperature is typically estimated by the oxygen isotope ratios measured in ice cores. If these paleotemperatures changed abruptly, by 5°C or so, they probably don't represent the average temperature, because the average ocean temperature could not change this much without a catastrophic cause. An underlying assumption of the Astronomical Theory is uniformitarianism.

It is likely that for these reasons and others that the Astronomical Theory is not a correct explanation for climate changes on the Earth and, therefore, oxygen isotope trends in ice and sea-floor sediment cores. Vardiman (1993) first suggested that major trends in oxygen isotope ratios in ice cores could be explained by the formation and decay of ice shelves on the polar oceans. Vardiman (1997) then presented a more complete treatment of this idea. This section will follow that treatment.

Ice Core Data

Figures 4.9, 4.10, and 4.11 show $\delta^{18}O$ and formation temperature as a function of depth for Camp Century, Dye-3, and Summit in Greenland, respectively. Uniform values of $\delta^{18}O$ have been consistently observed in the upper portion of the ice cores, with a minimum in the lower portion and a maximum at the very bottom. By assuming that the fractionation of the two isotopes of oxygen is proportional to the temperature at which precipitation is formed in the atmosphere, an historical trend in temperature near the earth's surface can be calculated. The estimated air temperatures are shown on the right sides of Figures 4.9, 4.10, and 4.11. The temperatures are calculated from Equation 4.2.

The relatively high values of $\delta^{18}O$ and therefore, high air temperatures at the very bottom of the cores, are thought to support the idea of a warm ocean prior to the last "Ice Age." The slow cooling of the warm ocean over about 100,000 years resulted in a glacial maximum near the minimum in $\delta^{18}O$. An, as yet, unexplained change in climate caused the rapid deglaciation and warming near the steep increase in $\delta^{18}O$ just to the right of the homogeneous upper portion of the cores. Because the lower portions of the ice sheets are greatly compressed by the weight of the ice above, the conventional interpretation of these data attributes long periods of time to the lower parts of the cores. Vardiman (1993) has reinterpreted the time model suggesting that high precipitation rates likely occurred following the Genesis Flood, shortening this time period greatly.

Because only minor changes in solar heating have been assumed in the past, the large cooling and heating in the ocean temperature inferred from Figures 4.9, 4.10, and 4.11 are

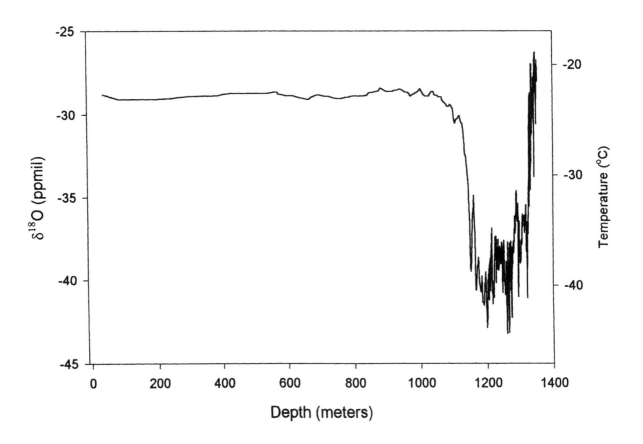

Figure 4.9 $\delta^{18}O$ vs. depth for Camp Century, Greenland.

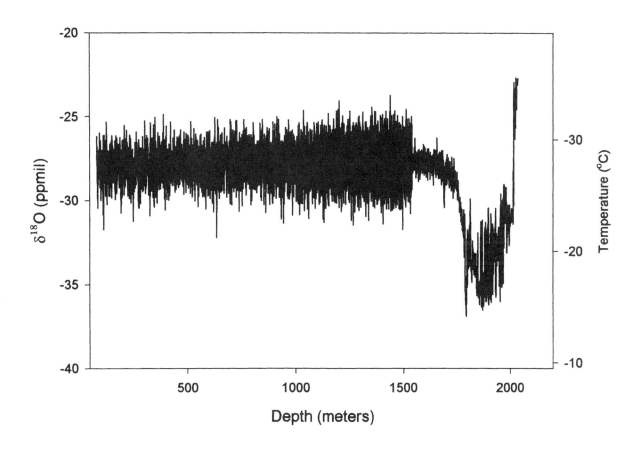

Figure 4.10 $\delta^{18}O$ *vs.* depth for Dye-3, Greenland.

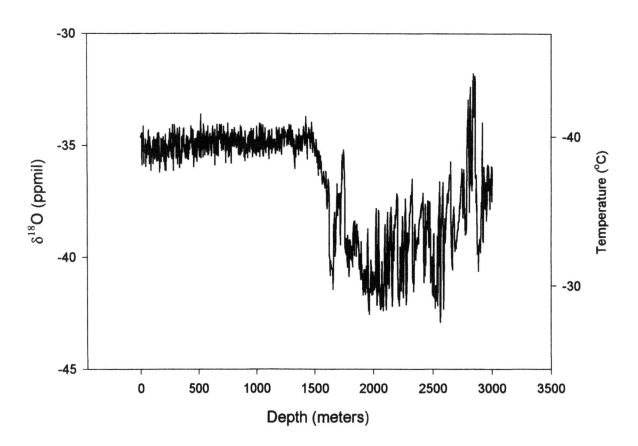

Figure 4.11   δ¹⁸O *vs.* depth for Summit, Greenland.

thought to require long periods of time. A decrease in ocean temperature produces a change in fractionation of the two types of oxygen, resulting in lower values of $\delta^{18}O$. The heavier isotope of oxygen, ^{18}O, is slower to evaporate into the atmosphere, leaving the ocean enriched in ^{18}O and the atmosphere depleted. When the atmospheric water vapor is subsequently precipitated as snow it exhibits low values of $\delta^{18}O$. In addition to this temperature effect, Bowen (1991) and Petit *et al.* (1991) have suggested that variations in the $\delta^{18}O$ of snow in polar regions may also be due to variations in $\delta^{18}O$ of the source, the distance from the evaporation source to the accumulation site, and the type of precipitation process which converts water vapor to snow in the atmosphere. Changes in the temperature of the condensation level and altitude effects due to topography can also affect $\delta^{18}O$. Although all of these processes are probably active in producing the trends observed in the ice cores, this section will address the effect of distance from the evaporation source on trends in $\delta^{18}O$ at the accumulation site.

A Young-earth Explanation for the Variation in Oxygen Isotopes in Ice Cores

The oceans are the primary source of water vapor for transport to the polar regions and precipitation as snow. The rate of evaporation from the open ocean is a function of the air-sea-surface temperature difference, atmospheric stability, and wind speed. The vapor pressure above a water surface is an exponential function of temperature, and the evaporation rate is closely related. The evaporation rate has been suggested by some to be proportional to the square of the wind speed across the ocean surface. The total function is often modeled as a product of these two relationships.

Following the Genesis Flood, as the oceans cooled and heavy snowfall occurred in the polar regions, it is likely that ice shelves began to develop slowly outward from the continents and equatorward from the poles. The greatest rate of ice shelf development probably occurred at the end of the "Ice Age." Formation of such ice shelves would cause a discontinuous decrease in evaporation of water vapor from the underlying ocean surfaces into the atmosphere. As these shelves grew equatorward the primary source of water vapor for snow formation was moved farther away from continental ice sheets where ice cores were later drilled. It is anticipated that the heaviest snowfall would typically occur near the edges of the ice shelves because of higher water vapor contents and dynamic effects. This greater mass of snow would fall from the lower portions of the clouds where warmer temperatures prevail. The number of ice crystals nucleated in a cloud is proportional to a negative exponential function of temperature. The higher and colder the location in a cloud, the greater the concentration, but the smaller the size, of the crystals formed. Small ice crystals fall more slowly than larger or more heavily rimed ones. Ice crystals become "rimed" when they fall through supercooled liquid cloud droplets. They collect the cloud droplets by collision and adhesion. The snowfall would be less intense and form higher and colder in the clouds farther away from the edges of the ice shelves. Because winds are typically stronger at higher altitudes, snow formed high in the clouds would also be transported longer distances before falling to the ground. Stronger updrafts near the edges of the ice shelves would also suspend smaller, slower-falling ice crystals.

If the fractionation of oxygen isotopes during the phase change from vapor to ice is proportional to temperature, as it is from liquid to vapor, $\delta^{18}O$ would be more negative the colder the temperature and the higher in the cloud the snow is formed. Therefore, the farther the edges of the ice shelves are from the accumulation sites, the more negative $\delta^{18}O$ would be. If $\delta^{18}O$ is interpreted to only be a result of the ocean temperature, it would then appear that the ocean has cooled dramatically to produce this effect. However, this trend could be a result of the greater distance from the source of evaporation beyond the edge of an ice shelf to the accumulation site as the ice shelves grew equatorward. The gradual decrease in $\delta^{18}O$ from the bottom of the ice cores to the minimum in $\delta^{18}O$ shown in Figures 4.9, 4.10, and 4.11 could be partially explained by an increasing distance from the source region to the accumulation site as the ice shelves grow. The change in $\delta^{18}O$ by this mechanism could occur much more rapidly than would be expected if the temperature of the entire ocean were required to change.

The sudden rebound in $\delta^{18}O$ to higher values above the minimum has typically been explained by the "deglaciation" brought about by some, as yet, unknown mechanism which produced sudden warming. However, recent evidence has shown that some events within this "deglaciation" occurred in an *extremely* short period of time. For example, in the steep portion of the curve, the "Younger Dryas" has been shown to have a period as short as four years (Alley *et al.*, 1992, 1993). If $\delta^{18}O$ is primarily a function of ocean temperature, then this rebound implies that the ocean surfaces warmed by as much as 20°C in a period of a few hundred years or less. No one has suggested a mechanism for such dramatic warming of the oceans.

The alternative to this scenario is the realization that the variation of $\delta^{18}O$ in Figures 4.9, 4.10, and 4.11 may be primarily due to the effect of ice shelves growing slowly equatorward and then suddenly melting, changing the distance between the evaporation source and the accumulation site. If most of the trend in $\delta^{18}O$ is assumed to be due to this effect, Figures 4.9, 4.10, and 4.11 can be used to estimate the average sea-surface temperature at the end of the Genesis Flood. The average global ocean temperature today is about 3.5°C, and the average global sea-surface temperature is about 18°C. If the amount of permanent ice cover on the oceans today is similar to that at the end of the Genesis Flood (not necessarily true), and the isotopic fractionation is proportional to the average sea-surface temperature, then the difference in $\delta^{18}O$ between the very oldest ice at the bottom of the ice cores and the homogeneous conditions of today should represent the temperature change between then and now. The difference appears to be about 4‰ or about 6°C. This means the average sea-surface temperature at the end of the Genesis Flood may have been about 24°C.

Precipitation Trajectories

Although the conceptual model of precipitation formation and isotope fractionation presented above would seem to agree with the trends of $\delta^{18}O$ observed in the ice cores, the case has yet to be made for the strength of the effects being of the correct magnitude. The ultimate test of this model is the calculation of predicted changes in $\delta^{18}O$ and agreement with the measured values.

The complete quantification of this model must await the development of better numerical models which can fully treat the vertical and horizontal wind fields, the formation of condensate in a cloud, the nucleation and growth of ice crystals, the fractionation of oxygen isotopes as a function of height and temperature in the cloud, and the fallout and transport of ice crystals to the ground as a function of distance from the edge of the ice shelf. However, a few crude calculations using the basic equations which describe the processes above will be reported here as a precursor to a more complete development to be attempted later.

The normal manner in which calculations would be made on precipitation formation and transport would be by the development of an Eulerian system of coordinates. In the Eulerian system, a set of boxes are defined through which the air and particles flow. A budget of water mass is maintained in each box and fluxes of condensate and precipitation particles through the top, bottom, and sides are computed. The final distribution of precipitation is the flux through the bottom layer of boxes. A reasonable set of dimensions would be 1,000 km in the horizontal direction in 5 km increments and 10 km in the vertical in 250 m increments. This would result in 2,000 boxes each 0.25 km high by 10 km on each side. The vertical dimensions would allow a small ice crystal to fall from 5 km to the ground in about 10 hours, during which time it would travel about 700 km horizontally in a 20 meter/second wind and still be within the grid. On the other hand, a large, heavily-rimed ice crystal could fall from 1 km to the ground in about 30 minutes and travel about 10 km horizontally in a 5 meter/second wind so that fine features of the precipitation distribution could be distinguished.

In the calculations to follow, however, a Lagrangian system of coordinates will be used. This system follows a single precipitation particle from nucleation to fallout on the ground as snow. The simple calculations in this approach will not consider mass balance nor permit a calculation of precipitation rate to be computed at the ground, but will allow easy visualization of the trajectories of the particles. Twelve particles starting from different positions in a typical wind field will be followed to demonstrate how the starting point influences the final fallout position, mass, and $\delta^{18}O$. Figure 4.12 shows the initial positions of the 12 particles as black dots and the assumed wind field in a vertical cross-section above and perpendicular to the ice shelf as arrows. The 12 starting positions are upwind of the ice shelf and representative of typical nucleation locations for ice crystals.

For these calculations, the wind field was assumed to be constant in time. However, the vertical and horizontal components vary in space relative to the edge of the ice shelf as shown at the bottom of Figure 4.12. The horizontal wind components are composed of two factors, one of which is dependent on the quadrant in the diagram and the other dependent on altitude. In all four quadrants the magnitude of the first factor of the horizontal wind component varies linearly from 0 meters/second at the outer boundaries (±800 km horizontally and 0 and 5 km vertically) to 5 meters/second at the center lines (0 km horizontally and 2.5 km vertically). The direction of the wind is to the right in the upper two quadrants and toward the edge of the ice shelf in the lower two quadrants (to the right in the lower left quadrant and to the left in the lower right quadrant).

This first factor in the horizontal wind is typical of the atmospheric flow relative to a surface thermal discontinuity, like what would be expected over warm water to the left of the edge of the ice shelf and ice to the right. Because of maximum upward motions near the edge of the ice shelf, air would normally converge at low levels and diverge aloft.

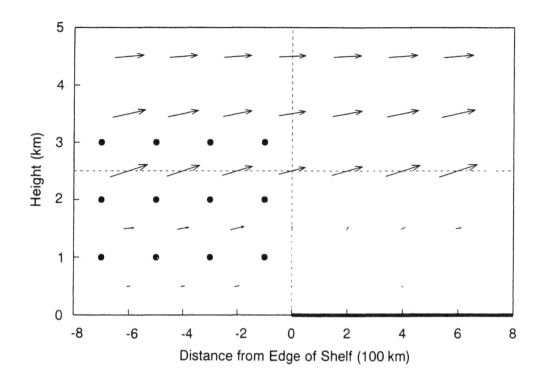

Figure 4.12   Initial position of 12 particles in a typical wind field.

The second factor in the horizontal wind is the general increase in wind from the surface upward. In this model the horizontal wind toward the right is assumed to increase linearly from 0 meters/second at the surface to 20 meters/second at 5 km in altitude. When these two factors are multiplied together the horizontal wind is nearly zero in the lower right-hand quadrant, as seen in Figure 4.12, and increases upward through both left-side quadrants. The upper right quadrant is almost uniform, with slightly stronger winds at 2.5 km.

The vertical wind field is similar to the first factor in the horizontal wind field, but the maximum upward velocity occurs at the edge of the ice shelf and at 2.5 km, and can be set to any desired value. This maximum value will be varied from 0.1 meters/second to 5 meters/second for this study. Synoptic-scale vertical motions are typically at the low end of this range. The value of the maximum vertical component of the wind field shown in Figure 4.12 is 5 meters/second. This general wind pattern is often observed near fronts in the atmosphere or surface thermal discontinuities. The wind field for this study was prescribed, but could be solved from the equations of motion using general boundary conditions.

Three types of ice crystals were assumed to be nucleated at each of the 12 starting positions. The position, mass, and $\delta^{18}O$ were calculated at 10-minute intervals as each crystal fell and drifted with the wind. The three types of crystals used were graupel, spatial dendrites, and planar crystals. Graupel are small hailstones that grow in strong convective updrafts with abundant supercooled water droplets. They have relatively high terminal velocities. Spatial dendrites are three-dimensional crystals with intermediate terminal velocities. Planar crystals are two-dimensional plates and dendrites with low terminal velocities. The diameter of each crystal was assumed to grow at the rate of 1 micrometer/second. This growth rate was assumed to be independent of crystal type, temperature, vapor pressure and crystal concentration. This is a very crude assumption and must obviously be treated more completely in future modeling. However, the numerical value of 1 micrometer/second is a reasonable average value shown by Ryan *et al.* (1976). The terminal velocity of these three crystal types re given by Mason (1971) as:

$$\text{Graupel:} \quad v_t = 0.5D \quad (4.26)$$

$$\text{Spatials:} \quad v_t = 0.35D \quad (4.27)$$

$$\text{Planars:} \quad v_t = 0.3 \quad (4.28)$$

where v_t is the terminal velocity in meters/second and D is the diameter of the crystal in millimeters.

The crystals were allowed to fall relative to the ground at a speed equal to the difference between the vertical component of the assumed wind at their location and their terminal velocities. They were allowed to drift horizontally with the horizontal component of the assumed wind. For stronger updrafts and slower falling crystals, the trajectories of the crystals were upward to the right, often drifting for long distances before reaching the ground. For weaker updrafts and faster falling crystals, the trajectories of the crystals were downward to the right. Even in very strong

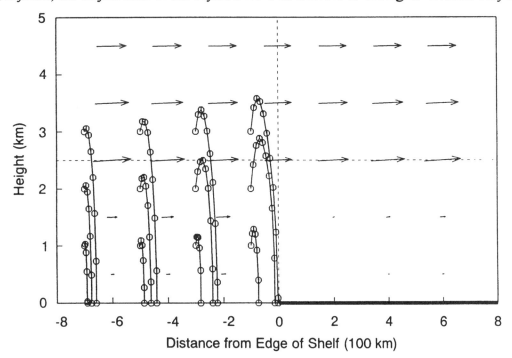

Figure 4.13   Trajectories of graupel in a 100 cm/sec maximum vertical wind.

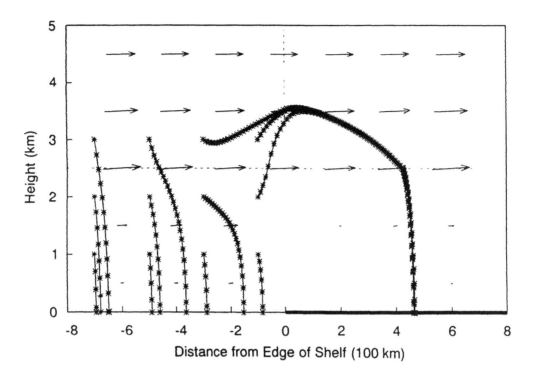

Figure 4.14 Trajectories of spatial crystals in a 100 cm/sec maximum vertical wind.

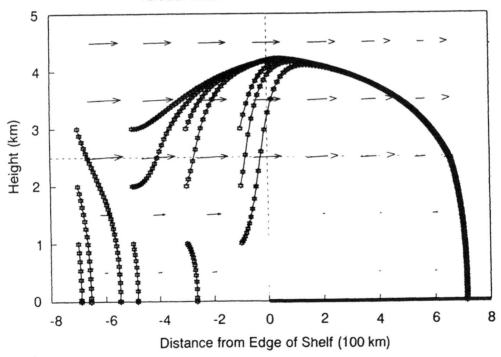

Figure 4.15 Trajectories of dendritic crystals in a 100 cm/sec maximum vertical wind.

updrafts, graupel often fell to the surface in short times and distances. Figures 4.13, 4.14, and 4.15 show the trajectories of the three crystal types for a maximum vertical wind component of 1 meter/second.

Notice for the wind field assumed in this study that graupel falls rapidly to the surface and drifts only a short distance downwind (see Figure 4.13). Spatials that form in the weaker vertical wind upwind of the ice shelf and at lower altitudes also fall rapidly to the surface and drift short distances downwind (see Figure 4.14). However, those which start closer to the edge of the ice shelf, where the vertical wind is stronger, are lofted upward and drift almost 500 km downwind before they reach the surface. Planars exhibit a similar pattern as spatials, but many more starting positions will permit crystals to be lofted and drift over 700 km downwind from the edge of the ice shelf (see Figure 4.15). It is interesting to note that those crystals which are lofted tend to reach the same location on the ground, even though they originate from different starting positions. This result is puzzling and should be confirmed in future research efforts.

Horizontal Dispersion of Oxygen Isotopes

Although the trajectories of ice crystals and their precipitation to the ground is interesting in its own right, the primary intent of this investigation is to determine the dispersion of $\delta^{18}O$ as a function of distance from the edge of an ice shelf. To find the dispersion of $\delta^{18}O$ downwind of the edge of an ice shelf we must compute the position and average $\delta^{18}O$ of each ice crystal when it reaches the surface. However, the average $\delta^{18}O$ of an ice crystal is strongly affected by both its mass rate of growth and the temperature where the growth occurs. The mass growth rate can be computed as a function of crystal diameter from Mason (1971) for each crystal type:

Graupel: $\quad m = 0.065 D^3$ \hfill (4.29)

Spatials: $\quad m = 0.010 D^2$ \hfill (4.30)

Planars: $\quad m = 0.0038 D^2$ \hfill (4.31)

where m is the mass of a crystal in milligrams and D is the diameter in millimeters.

Numerous researchers report on laboratory and field studies of the fractionation of oxygen isotopes by evaporation from a water surface. However, relatively few deal with the complex process of evaporation from the ocean to fallout as snow. Craig (1961, 1965), Dansgaard (1964), Johnsen *et al.* (1989), Jouzel and Marlivat (1984), Jouzel *et al.* (1982, 1987), and Petit *et al.* (1991) report on the fractionation of oxygen isotopes during the phase change from liquid to vapor. They determined that $\delta^{18}O$ in the evaporated water vapor by measuring the $\delta^{18}O$ in the residual liquid following a period of evaporation. Johnsen *et al.* (1989) used the relationship in Equation 4.2 between air temperature and $\delta^{18}O$ assuming evaporation from the oceans, transport to the polar regions, and deposition as snow (a phase change from vapor to ice). If this relationship is applied to our calculation for a phase change from vapor to ice, where T is the temperature at which the ice crystal is growing, we can calculate $\delta^{18}O$ of the most recent layer of ice growth. This is also an approximation which will need refinement in future efforts. If we also know the mass of the most recent growth from Equations 4.29, 4.30, and 4.31, we can find the average $\delta^{18}O$ from nucleation to the current position. This calculation will require the vertical temperature distribution in the atmosphere to be prescribed. For this study a surface temperature of 0°C and a lapse rate of 6.4°C/km, the moist adiabatic, was assumed. $\delta^{18}O$ of a crystal varies as the crystal grows and moves through different temperature levels. Once it precipitates onto the surface it remains unchanged. The average $\delta^{18}O$ from nucleation to fallout by mass-averaging is calculated as follows:

$$\overline{\delta^{18}O} = \frac{\int_0^M \delta^{18}O\, dm}{\int_0^M dm} \quad (4.32)$$

where dm is the infinitesimal amount of mass added to a crystal at any stage in the growth process, M is the total mass of a crystal when it reaches the surface, $\delta^{18}O$ is the oxygen isotope ratio of the added mass, and $\overline{\delta^{18}O}$ is the average oxygen isotope ratio of the crystal when it reaches the surface.

Figure 4.16 shows the dispersion of $\overline{\delta^{18}O}$ using this method. $\overline{\delta^{18}O}$ is plotted as a function of distance from the edge of the ice shelf for each of the three crystal types. In order to fill the domain of this plot the trajectories for the 12 starting positions shown in Figure 4.12 were computed for the three crystal types with maximum vertical velocities between 0.1 and 5.0 meters/second.

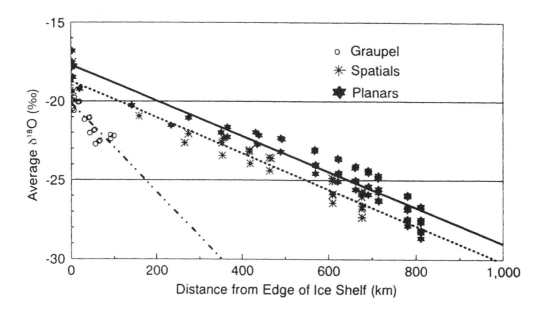

Figure 4.16   Dispersion of $\delta^{18}O$ vs. distance from edge of ice shelf.

$\overline{\delta^{18}O}$ is found to be inversely proportional to the distance from the edge of an ice shelf. The farther downwind the precipitation occurs the lower the value of $\overline{\delta^{18}O}$. This relationship is strongest for ice crystals which have the smallest terminal velocities. Graupel have the weakest dispersion of $\overline{\delta^{18}O}$ over distance because the trajectories are so steep that they remain in the upper atmosphere at cold temperatures for only a brief time. They do not acquire low average values of $\overline{\delta^{18}O}$. The data near the left-hand side of Figure 4.16 are produced by lower vertical wind velocities, and those on the right side by higher velocities. It is evident that two of the most important parameters for the dispersion of $\overline{\delta^{18}O}$ are crystal type and vertical wind velocity.

The values of $\overline{\delta^{18}O}$ were computed strictly from Equation 4.2. No consideration was given to the variation of $\overline{\delta^{18}O}$ as a function of latitude, height, or difference between the time of the Flood and today. Although some investigators have reported strong variation of $\overline{\delta^{18}O}$ in snow as a function of location, it is not known if this is due to space and time changes or to the effect explored in this paper. It is likely that if the Flood was as catastrophic as suggested by some, large variations in $\overline{\delta^{18}O}$ of the precipitation would be expected with time, at least initially.

Application to Ice Shelves

It appears that we now have a powerful mechanism for explaining the oxygen isotope trends in ice cores. If an ice core is drilled through an ice sheet on Greenland or Antarctica, it contains the record of $\delta^{18}O$ which precipitated at a given location. If the site of the ice core was a short distance from the open ocean (say 200 km) at the time the snow at the bottom of the ice core fell, the value of $\delta^{18}O$ would be about -18‰ according to Figure 4.16. However, if an ice shelf was forming over the open ocean so that the distance was slowly increasing to 1,000 km or so, the value of $\delta^{18}O$ would decrease to about -28‰.

Furthermore, if a sudden reversal in the growth of the ice shelf occurred, causing the distance to decrease rapidly to 400 km or so, the value of $\delta^{18}O$ would increase rapidly to -23‰. If the shelf were to remain fixed at a constant distance from the ice core site, the trend in $\delta^{18}O$ would approximate the trend observed in the upper portion of the ice cores as shown in Figures 4.9, 4.10, and 4.11. It is interesting that Camp Century is the farthest north and likely had the longest trajectory over an ice shelf. $\delta^{18}O$ exhibits the greatest change at Camp Century. The ice cores from Dye or Summit should produce a similar trend, but the magnitude of $\delta^{18}O$ would probably be different. The distance from the open ocean to the core site must be taken into account. The real atmospheric wind fields have also not been considered. Many of the assumed relationships in this first model will probably need major revision when applied to different locations.

Conclusions and Recommendations

It would appear that this simple, first model for the dispersion of $\delta^{18}O$ as a function of distance from the edge of a growing or retreating ice shelf has been successful in providing an alternative explanation for the observed oxygen isotope trends in ice cores. We can tentatively conclude that a major portion of the slow decrease in $\delta^{18}O$ with time during the early portions of the latest "Ice Age," followed by a rapid increase in $\delta^{18}O$ during the deglaciation, could be due to the slow growth and subsequent rapid melting of an ice shelf on the upwind ocean rather than slow cooling and re-warming of the ocean itself.

It is also evident that much work remains to be done to improve these calculations. Only simple average relationships were used. Prescriptive rather than prognostic wind fields were used. More complete cloud physics should be incorporated. An Eulerian as well as Lagrangian trajectory system should be modeled. The relation between temperature and oxygen isotope fractionation during a phase change from vapor to ice should be improved. The magnitude of $\delta^{18}O$ near the bottoms of various cores, at the "Ice Age" minima of $\delta^{18}O$, and at the uniform upper portions of the cores, should be correlated with distance from the ocean, dynamics, and cloud physics to determine if this information will provide insights into the boundary conditions.

Finally, if the growth and retreat of ice shelves is an adequate explanation for $\delta^{18}O$ trends in ice cores, 100,000 years is no longer needed to explain the "Ice Age." Vardiman (1993) has already developed an adequate explanation for the accumulation of large quantities of ice in polar regions over short periods of time. The growth and decay of ice shelves could also occur over short periods of time, permitting the young-earth model of the "Ice Age" to explain the trends in $\delta^{18}O$ of ice cores.

CHAPTER 5

SEA-FLOOR SEDIMENT ACCUMULATION

Introduction

During the development of the young-earth time model for ice cores described by Vardiman (1993) it was realized that a similar development was needed for sea-floor sediment. Vardiman (1996) reported on such a study.

The conventional paleoclimatological community has extended the Astronomical Theory over tens of "Ice Ages" by interpreting the variations of $\delta^{18}O$ in sea-floor sediments in terms of climate change. It has been demonstrated that when the $\delta^{18}O$ in the ocean decreases, $\delta^{18}O$ in polar ice increases and vice versa. This inverse relationship is thought to be due to the conservation of mass between the two reservoirs of liquid and solid water. Because sea-floor sediments contain many more oscillations of $\delta^{18}O$ than polar ice sheets it is thought to extend back in time millions of years.

Figure 5.1 shows the variation of $\delta^{18}O$ in a sea-floor sediment core from the equatorial Pacific. The saw-toothed peaks are believed to each represent an "Ice Age." This core is thought to extend back in time over 700,000 years and contain evidence for at least seven "Ice Ages." Note that the first oscillation, closest to the sea floor, is believed to mirror the variation in $\delta^{18}O$ in the ice cores shown in Figures 4.9, 4.10, and 4.11.

The time frame offered by the conventional explanation of climate suggest that the ocean sediments accumulated over hundreds of millions of years, and recent "Ice Ages" occurred over periods of time on the order of a hundred millennia. These ages are not compatible with a literal interpretation of the Biblical account of creation and earth history. The main sources of disagreement between the conventional model of earth history and a model consistent with the Bible for sediment accumulation are those about the magnitude of the driving mechanism and the process rates. The conventional model assumes sediment accumulated slowly over long periods of time by low-energy processes. The creation model assumes sediment accumulated rapidly over a relatively short period of time by catastrophic processes during and following the global Flood described in Genesis.

It is evident from geology that if the Flood was global and recent, it would not have been a tranquil event. The inference is that the Flood waters moved across the surface of the earth and eroded miles of the surface sediments and rocks into fine sands and muds. These sediments were deposited primarily on what are continents today. Only minor quantities of sediment were deposited on the ocean floor compared to the continents. Most of the sediments lower in the geologic column beneath the oceans are completely missing. Volcanoes, eruptions of magma, earthquakes, continental movements, tidal waves, continual rain, mountain building, and massive erosion of canyons and plains contributed to the devastation. Forests were destroyed, vegetation and animals were buried, and massive fossil graveyards were created all over the earth as the waters subsided and the suspended sands and muds settled out of the seas.

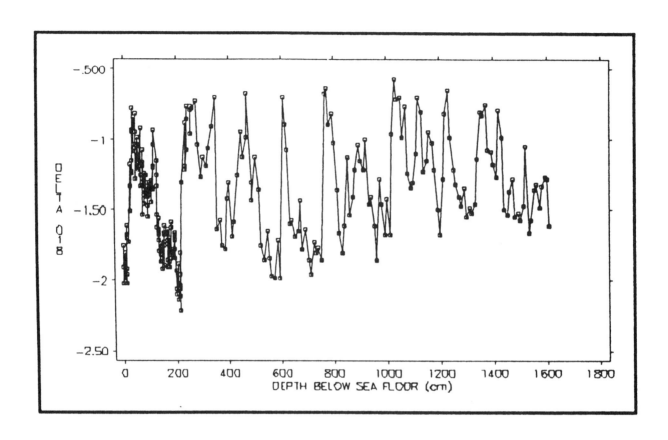

Figure 5.1 $\delta^{18}O$ in sea-floor sediments *vs.* depth for site V28-238 in the equatorial Pacific

As the continents rose and the sea floors sank at the end of the Flood to form a new isostatic adjustment of the earth's crust, some of the unconsolidated sediments were eroded off the continents into the oceans and settled on the floor close to the continental boundaries (See Wise *et al.*, 1994). The continental sediments solidified into rock (lithification) forming the sedimentary rocks observed all over the earth today. On the ocean floor the deeper sediments lithified under the influence of higher pressures and temperatures which removed or chemically altered the water present in the sediments. The ocean floor is much thinner (5-10 kilometers thick) and therefore closer to the heat of the mantle than the continents (35-60 kilometers thick). Water was drained from the sediments on the continents by gravity, aiding the lithification. The water remaining in the oceans may have been chemically altered as well.

The upper layers of sediment on the ocean floor were formed after the Flood as warm, nutrient-rich oceans "bloomed" with forams, radiolaria, coccoliths, diatoms, and many other forms of microscopic and macroscopic life. The ocean floor was littered with shells and debris of life forms living, growing, and dying in abundance. This debris was mixed with residual lithogenous sediments immediately after the Flood because of barren surfaces, unlithified sediments, and greater precipitation than today. The amount of sediments entering and forming in the ocean decreased markedly with time after the Flood. It is possible that the warmth of the ocean and possible heating of the floor below caused rapid oxidation which produced the red and brown muds.

The conventional old-earth age model assigns an age of about 65 million years BP to the end of the Cretaceous period. A literal interpretation of Scripture would suggest that the origin of planet earth occurred quite recently -- much less than 65 million years ago. The recent-creation age model assumes God created the world in a supernatural creative event some 6 - 10,000 years ago, and judged his creation through a worldwide catastrophic Flood some 4,500 years ago. The assumption that the Flood occurred about 4,500 years ago is derived from the Ussher (1786) chronology using the Textus Receptus. Between God's supernatural interventions in the affairs of the world, God normally allows the physical processes to operate according to the laws of science. We wish to determine whether the sea-floor sediment data can be reasonably explained within this conceptual framework.

A Young-earth Age Model

The conventional age model used to calculate the age of sediments as a function of depth assumes that the accumulation rate of sediment was essentially constant over millions of years at today's average rate of about 2×10^{-5} meters/year. If, in fact, the accumulation rate was much greater following the Flood and decreased exponentially until today, then the period of time back to the formation of a given layer can be found by the following sediment accumulation model.

Following Vardiman (1996) let the sediment accumulation rate be an exponentially decreasing function of time since the Flood:

$$\frac{dy}{dt} = Ae^{-\frac{t}{\tau}} \qquad \text{5.1}$$

where y represents the height of a sediment layer above a reference point (in this case, the Cretaceous/Tertiary boundary), A is a constant to be determined from the boundary conditions, τ the relaxation time, and t the time after the Flood when a layer of sediment was laid down.

This equation can be integrated to give the height y directly:

$$y = -A\tau e^{-\frac{t}{\tau}} + C \qquad \text{5.2}$$

where C represents a constant of integration to be determined from the boundary conditions. For the first boundary condition, $y = 0$ at $t = 0$. No sediment had yet begun to accumulate, so:

$$y = 0 = -A\tau + C \qquad \text{5.3}$$

Solving for C and substituting into Eq. 5.2:

$$y = A\tau[1 - e^{-\frac{t}{\tau}}] \qquad 5.4$$

For the second boundary condition, $y = H$ at $t = t_F$, where H represents the total depth of the sediment above the Cretaceous/Tertiary boundary and t_F is the time in years since the Flood. For this condition:

$$y(t = t_F) = H = A\tau[1 - e^{-\frac{t_F}{\tau}}] \qquad 5.5$$

Solving for A:

$$A = \frac{H}{\tau[1 - e^{-\frac{t_F}{\tau}}]} \qquad 5.6$$

Substituting back into Eq. 5.4:

$$y = \frac{H[e^{\frac{t}{\tau}} - 1]}{[e^{\frac{t}{\tau}} - \frac{e^{-\frac{t_F}{\tau}}}{e^{-\frac{t}{\tau}}}]} \qquad 5.7$$

A more useful relationship may be found by inverting this equation to find t as a function of y, H, and τ.

$$t = -\tau \ln[1 - \frac{y}{H}(1 - e^{-\frac{t_F}{\tau}})] \qquad 5.8$$

This relationship is typically called an age model and is used to find the age of a layer based on its vertical position. At this point, it is not specific to any particular worldview and can be applied to any chronology by substituting any time frame, t_F, between the Cretaceous/Tertiary boundary and today.

If the chronology of the Biblical events according to Ussher (1786) is assumed to be true, approximately 4,500 years have transpired since the Flood ($t_F = 4,500$). Using this time interval, the average observed depth of sea-floor above the Cretaceous/Tertiary boundary (322 meters), and the measured accumulation rate of sediment today (2×10^{-5} meters/year), the relaxation time, τ, may be determined from Eqs. 5.1 and 5.5.

Substituting the time interval since the Flood and today's sediment accumulation rate into Eq. 5.1:

$$\frac{dy}{dt}(t = 4500) = Ae^{-\frac{4500}{\tau}} = 2 \times 10^{-5} m/yr \qquad 5.9$$

The initial sedimentation rate, A, in terms of the relaxation time, τ, may be found:

$$A = (2 \times 10^{-5} m/yr) e^{\frac{4500}{\tau}} \qquad 5.10$$

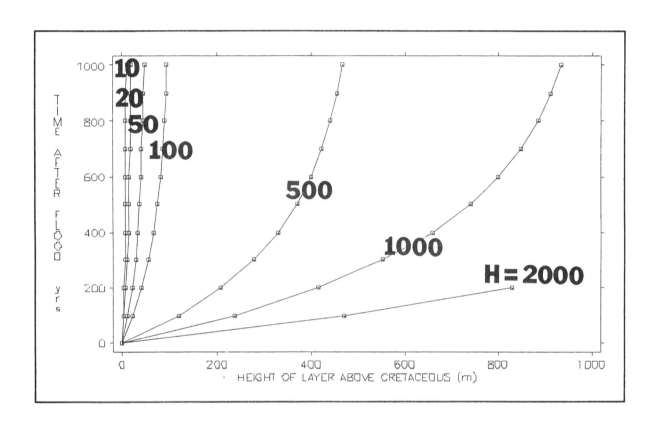

Figure 5.2 Age of a sediment layer from the young-earth model *vs.* height above the Cretaceous/Tertiary boundary for various values of the total sediment depth, H, in meters

Substituting *A* into Eq. 5.5:

$$H = (2x10^{-5} m/yr)\tau[e^{\frac{4500}{\tau}} - 1] \qquad \textbf{5.11}$$

Rewriting in order to facilitate solving for τ:

$$\ln[1 + \frac{H}{2x10^{-5}\tau}] = \frac{4500}{\tau} \qquad \textbf{5.12}$$

This is a transcendental equation in τ. The solution for τ can be found using iterative methods or by finding the point at which the two sides of the equation are satisfied jointly. The second method was used here by plotting the left and right sides of Eq. 5.12 simultaneously and solving for τ using the average value of *H*. The solution to this transcendental equation gives a value for τ of 373 years.

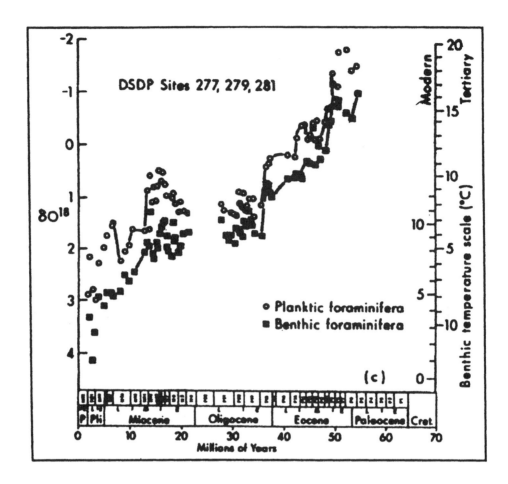

Figure 5.3 δ¹⁸O in sea-floor sediment *vs.* conventional time from DSDP sites 277, 279, and 281. (After Kennett *et al.*, 1977)

Substituting τ =373 years and t_F = 4,500 years into Eq. 5.8 results in the following young-earth age model, derived from young-earth boundary conditions:

$$t = -[373 years]\ln[1 - \frac{y}{H}(1 - e^{-\frac{4500 years}{373 years}})] \qquad 5.13$$

This age model is displayed in Figure 5.2. The height of sea-floor sediment above the Cretaceous/Tertiary boundary, *y*, is shown on the horizontal axis and time since the Flood, *t*, on the vertical axis. The age model is shown for several total sediment depths, *H*. Note, that each curve asymptotically approaches the value of *H* as time approaches 4,500 years after the Flood. In general, it can be seen from Eq. 5.7 that *y = 0* when *t = 0* and *y = H* when $t = t_F$.

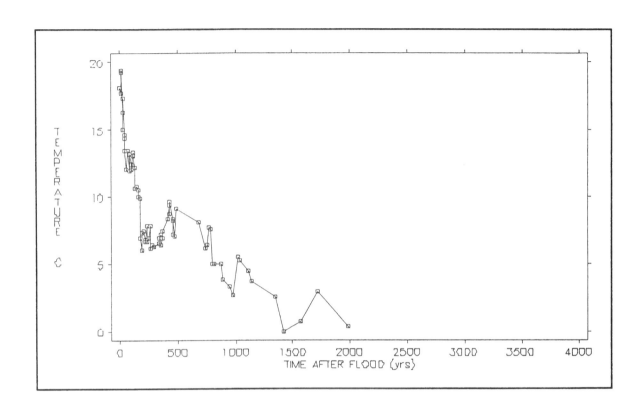

Figure 5.4   Paleotemperature derived from $\delta^{18}O$ in sea-floor sediment *vs.* young-earth time from DSDP sites 277, 279, and 281.

Applications of a Young-earth Age Model

The age model developed here can now be applied to data used by Kennett et al. (1977), plotted in Figure 5.3, to estimate ocean temperatures as a function of time from the Cretaceous to the present. Documentation of the operations, lithology, and biostratigraphy for DSDP sites 277, 279, and 281 are summarized in appendix E of Vardiman (1996). The analytical procedures are contained in Shackleton and Kennett (1975). For this analysis the total sediment depth, H, above the Cretaceous/Tertiary boundary was found to be 760 meters. Figure 5.4 shows the results of applying the new young-earth age model to these same data.

A significantly different interpretation of the data from that of Kennett et al. (1977) results. First, the period over which the data occur is assumed to be about 2 thousand years, rather than 65 million years. Second, the temperature initially decreases rapidly, followed by a slower decrease. The decrease shown by Kennett et al. (1977) is basically linear with a few short-period departures implying a gradual cooling over a long period of time. The trend shown in Figure 5.4 is typical of rapid cooling driven by a large temperature gradient. If the oceans were initially warm at the end of the Flood and were cooled to a new equilibrium temperature by radiation to space in the polar regions, this would be the type of cooling curve one would expect. The relaxation time appears to be about 1 thousand years.

This curve was derived from benthic forams in the South Pacific at high latitudes, so polar ocean bottom waters show dramatic cooling. Similar analysis of polar surface waters using planktic forams show a similar trend but average about 1 degree warmer. Equatorial surface waters show only a minor cooling of 5 degrees or so while equatorial bottom temperatures show a similar trend as polar waters.

These results are interpreted as surface cooling of polar waters followed by sinking and movement toward the equator along the ocean floor. A general oceanic circulation is established where warm equatorial water is transported poleward at the surface and cold polar water is transported toward the equator at the ocean floor. Horizontal gyres within the separate ocean basins are superimposed on these latitudinal motions by the Coriolis force.

In the polar regions one would expect surface cooling to decrease the temperatures at the ocean floor because the cooler water aloft would sink and displace the warmer water below. This interchange would result in vigorous vertical mixing and cooling of bottom waters. During this strong cooling period one would predict outstanding conditions for nutrient supply and formation of biogenous sediments in the polar regions. In the tropics the ocean would have become more stratified with time because of the advection of cold bottom water under the warmer surface water. Except for specific regions of upwelling along the continents and near the equatorial countercurrents, vertical transport of nutrients and, therefore, the formation of biogenous sediments, would have been more restricted.

The data resolution in Figure 5.4 is very coarse. Near the top of the sediments sampling must occur at close intervals for the young-earth model because the sedimentation rate is decreasing exponentially. Fortunately, many cores have been extracted in recent years and sampled for $\delta^{18}O$ at very high resolution. This allows time to be resolved to short intervals near the top of the core.

Figure 5.5 shows the results of applying the new young-earth age model to a high-resolution core from site RC11-120 in the SubAntarctic Pacific at about 45° S latitude. Note, that a consistent warming trend of about 5°C has occurred in the recent past preceded by rapid fluctuations at various time scales. Rapid warming followed by a slow cooling trend occurred between 1500 and 2500 years after the Flood. The "Ice Age" in the young-earth chronology would have ended about 2000 years ago. This event has been identified in the literature as the most recent "Ice Age" followed by rapid deglaciation. Note, that the period of this event is on the order of 700 years for the young-earth model instead of the conventional 100,000 years.

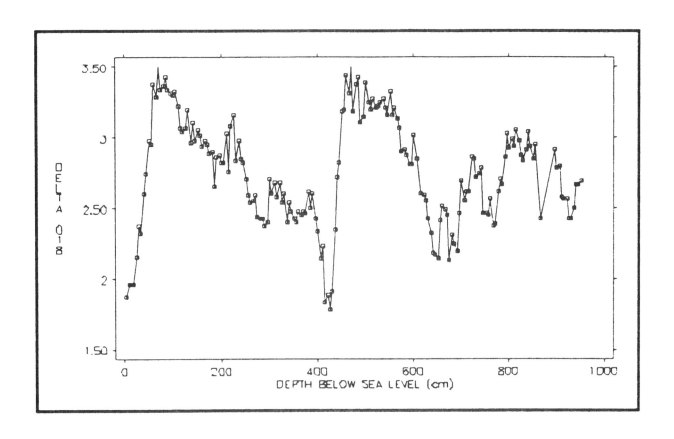

Figure 5.5   Polar ocean bottom temperature *vs.* time after the Flood. Data are from core RC11-120 used in the CLIMAP Project.

The young-earth age model has also been applied to a second high-resolution core shown in Figure 5.6. This core was taken from site V28-238 in the Pacific near the equator (the same core displayed using the conventional age model in Figure 5.1). The results show a 5°C warming trend in the recent past preceded by similar oscillations in temperature as Figure 5.5. The period of the feature in this core associated with the most recent "Ice Age" is also about 700 years, but the temperature is about 15°C warmer. Because this core was longer than the previous one we can see a longer period of temperature oscillations into the past. Notice that these oscillations have a fairly uniform period of about 100 years. This compares to a period of about 20 thousand years derived from the conventional age model.

Implications of a Young-earth Age Model

It has been recognized for several years that sediments on the ocean floor have been laid down in such a manner that some type of harmonic process has occurred. Analysis of $\delta^{18}O$ in fine

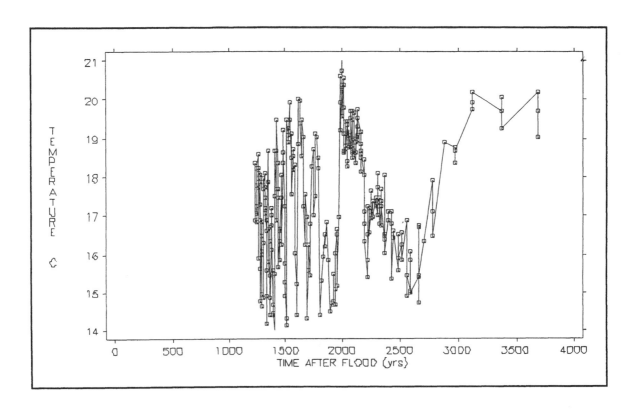

Figure 5.6   Equatorial Pacific ocean surface temperature *vs.* time after the Flood. Data are from core V28-238 used in the CLIMAP Project.

resolution cores shows periodic repetitions of cold and warm periods. A statistical correlation between the temperature oscillations and the periods of the three orbital parameters of the earth/sun system has led to strong support for the Astronomical Theory. CLIMAP (1976, 1981) and SPECMAP were two research projects designed to strengthen the evidence for this relationship.

A frequency analysis of many cores with the conventional age model found that peaks in the frequency spectra occurred at periods of approximately 20, 40, and 100 thousand years. Because these periods were similar to those of the orbital parameters, it has been assumed that the driving mechanism for the temperature fluctuations derived from sea-floor sediments is the change in radiational warming of the earth as the earth/sun distance and orientation change. These concepts have become known as the Astronomical Theory, a revision of a theory first proposed by Milankovich (1930, 1941).

However, several difficulties have yet to be resolved with this theory. First, the magnitude of the change in radiational heating calculated from the orbital parameters does not seem to be large enough to explain the observed cooling and heating. Secondary feedback mechanisms have been proposed to amplify the orbital effects. However, it has also been found that many of the hypothetical feedback mechanisms are of the wrong sign at certain phases in the orbital cycles.

A major result of this need for feedback mechanisms has been the development of a perspective that the earth's climate system is extremely sensitive to minor disturbances. A relatively minor perturbation could initiate a non-linear response which might lead to another "Ice Age" or "Greenhouse." Because of the fear that a small perturbation might lead to serious consequences, radical environmental policies on the release of smoke, chemicals, and other pollutants and the cutting of trees have been imposed by international agencies and some countries. If the basis for the Astronomical Theory is wrong, many of the more radical environmental efforts may be unjustified.

A second difficulty with the Astronomical Theory is the relative effect of the orbital parameters. The orbital parameter which has a period of about 100 thousand years and is associated with the 100 thousand-year-long "Ice Ages" produces the weakest changes in radiational heating. If the "Ice Ages" are caused by radiational changes, the orbital parameter causing them should be the largest of the three. Yet, the orbital parameter with the 100-thousand year period is the smallest of the three.

If the young-earth age model proposed by this work is valid, the correlation between sea-floor sediments and the orbital parameters is completely false. The periods illustrated in Figures 5.5 and 5.6 are on the order of 100 years and 700 years. Rather than an external forcing function like orbital parameters causing fluctuations in the earth's climate system, it is suggested that these oscillations are a manifestation of frequencies which are naturally present in the earth-atmosphere-ocean system. These natural frequencies were probably excited by the initial high-energy events of the Flood. In the young-earth model there has been only enough time for one "Ice Age" since the Flood. The initial forcing function for the "Ice Age" was the tremendous amount of heat left in the oceans by the events of the Flood. The length of the "Ice Age" would have been determined by the amount of time for the oceans to lose their heat to the atmosphere and subsequently to space.

Many other shorter-period oscillations in the earth's climate system may still be operating, however. For example, a significant oscillating climate event which has received a large amount of international research attention recently is the El Nino/Southern Oscillation (ENSO) which has been documented in the equatorial Pacific (Jacobs *et al.*, 1994). This oscillation has become known popularly as the El Nino/La Nina weather oscillation on the West Coast of North and South America. This climate event starts as a warming of surface waters in the western equatorial Pacific. It progresses eastward over a period of 2-4 years increasing precipitation along the equator and changing the wind patterns. When it intersects the Americas, it produces flooding and major changes in marine habitats along the west coasts of both continents. Effects further east cause wet and dry regions over large areas. This oscillation has a period of about 7 years and may be just one example of many such oscillations still observable in our atmosphere/ocean system.

If a young-earth age model of sea-floor sediment accumulation such as that developed in this research can be justified, then the conventional theories of multiple "Ice Ages," greenhouse warming, and millions of years of earth history required for evolutionary processes will be refuted. There seems to be no middle ground between the young-earth and old-earth models when treating the accumulation of sea-floor sediments.

CHAPTER 6

GLOBAL CLIMATE MODELING WITH CCM1

Introduction

The catastrophic events of the Flood described in Genesis 6-9 are almost unimaginable. In order for man and all land-breathing animals to have been destroyed in the Flood, the entire surface of the earth must have been devastated. The layers of sedimentary rock covering most of the earth, containing millions of fossils, are mute testimony to this event. Scripture says that flood waters covered all the mountains. If this was the case, many other major geological events also occurred: mountains rose up; valleys were carved out by receding flood waters; volcanoes spewed lava and dust over vast areas; forests were buried; and earthquakes and tidal waves swept the earth. Even the continents may have been broken apart during or shortly following the Flood.

The amount of energy released during these events would have resulted in significant warming of the oceans as noted by Oard (1986, p. 158; 1990, pp. 23-31) and Wise *et al.* (1994, p. 613). Heat released by the collapse of the waters above the earth and by magma from within the earth would probably have raised the average temperature of the oceans by tens of degrees above that of today. Not only would the oceans have been warmer, but because of all the mixing by the Flood, they probably would have been relatively uniform in temperature from top to bottom and from equator to pole. This is not true today. The oceans are colder near the poles and at the bottom.

The Biblical description of the pre-Flood world gives the impression of a relatively warm environment, with no rain or storms. If this is true, it is likely that no ice sheets existed at the poles prior to the Flood. However, even if they were in existence before the Flood, they would have melted or have been destroyed during the Flood. In polar regions today, vast sedimentary rock layers exist below the ice and extend upward in isolated outcrops called nunataks, testifying to the worldwide effects of the Flood.

Following the main deluge, many of the geologic processes did not cease abruptly, but, rather, decreased slowly in intensity and frequency, much like aftershocks following a major earthquake. Volcanoes probably continued to release dust and gases into the upper atmosphere for many years after the Flood, causing a pall over the entire earth. The observation of high concentrations of calcium, magnesium, and silicon in the lowest layers of ice cores taken from Greenland may be a reflection of these residual volcanic eruptions. This cover of volcanic dust and gases probably affected the radiation balance over the earth, causing greater cooling over continents and polar regions than we experience today.

The contrast between warm oceans and cold continents probably resulted in intense storminess along coastlines. A description of the effects of the Flood on the formation of an "Ice Age" is described by Oard (1990). He discusses in great detail causes of an "Ice Age;" the beginning, progression, and ending of an "Ice Age;" and evidences for a single "Ice Age," rather than many. However, Oard (1990) does not treat the evidence gleaned from ice cores, which would support such an alternative model, nor does he describe in detail the general circulation of the atmosphere which would likely be associated with such a model.

The General Circulation of Today's Atmosphere

The general circulation of the atmosphere, as it is observed and understood today, is shown in Figure 6.1. It is essentially the global movement of air on a rotating earth in response to differential heating of the equator and poles and the Coriolis force as described by Lorenz (1967). The earth's atmosphere is observed to be in thermal equilibrium, but net radiational cooling occurs at high latitudes near the poles and net warming occurs in the tropics and subtropics near the equator. To balance the thermal heat source near the equator with the heat sinks near the poles, the ocean and atmosphere transport heat from the tropics to high latitudes. This heat transfer is the driving force for weather and climate on the earth.

The circulating cells in the atmosphere nearest the equator cause air to rise over the equator and flow toward the poles, then descend near 30° latitude in both hemispheres. In the northern hemisphere, air is deflected to the right of its path by the Coriolis force, so that the northeast trade winds are created near the surface as the descending air moves back toward the equator. In the rising air near the equator, clouds form and heavy precipitation falls along a belt around the globe called the intertropical convergence zone, or the equatorial low. Near 30° latitude, where the air routinely descends, few, if any, clouds form, and desert conditions persist in a belt surrounding the earth. The region is a subtropical high.

Between the subtropical highs and the polar fronts further toward the poles, westerlies prevail. In the northern hemisphere this region is characterized by winds blowing from west to east, as surface air moves north from the subtropical high and is deflected to the right. It is also characterized by stormy weather, particularly in winter, as storms circle the globe along the polar front. Near the pole, air descends, as heat is removed by radiation to space. The cold air at the surface moves southward toward the polar front and is deflected to the right forming polar easterlies. Under the polar high, relatively few clouds and little precipitation form. A typical station in central Greenland today accumulates the equivalent of one foot of water per year in the form of ice and snow. What precipitation does occur remains in a frozen state for long periods of time.

Now, how would this picture likely have been different during and following the Flood when nonequilibrium conditions prevailed? If the oceans were uniformly warm from the equator to the poles and large temperature gradients existed from ocean to land, how would the general circulation have responded? We realize through recent field research that warmer oceans energize midlatitude storms and increase precipitation by what is called, "The El Niño Effect." If more moisture is evaporated into the atmosphere and the atmospheric circulation is more intense, could the polar ice caps have formed rapidly immediately following the Flood?

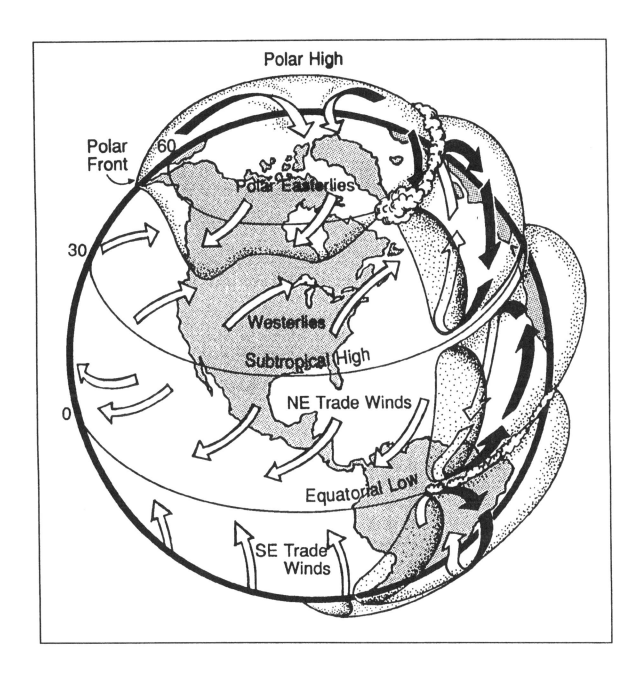

Figure 6.1   The general circulation of today's atmosphere. Light arrows show air flow at the surface and dark arrows aloft.

Climate Modeling

The use of climate modeling has grown tremendously in the 1980's and 90's. The need for computer climate models arose out of a desire for scientists to understand better global climate patterns. There is no doubt that the climate has changed throughout the earth's history. With the understanding that climate does fluctuate, climate models have been used in an effort to better understand paleoclimates and make more accurate predictions about future climates.

The ideal climate model represents the interaction between the atmosphere, ocean, and cryosphere, or regions on the earth's surface, where freezing temperatures exist. To date, even the best models fall short of this demand. Early climate models were one-dimensional and involved a single mechanism, such as heat energy entering and leaving the atmosphere. These energy balance models, although simple in structure, are popular because they are useful in examining just one aspect of the atmosphere and are inexpensive to operate since they run on a wider variety of computers and require less time to operate.

Another major classification is the general circulation model, or GCM. A GCM is a three-dimensional atmospheric circulation model. These numerical models operate according to specified nonlinear, three-dimensional, partial differential equations. The equations, based on the laws of classical physics, integrate the atmospheric variables over time. The basic equations are derived from Newton's second law of motion, the conservation of mass, and the conservation of energy. Other relationships like the hydrostatic equation, the ideal gas law, and the second law of thermodynamics are used to simplify the equations. The complete set of hydrodynamic equations in Cartesian coordinates for a nonviscous adiabatic atmosphere are shown in Eqs. 6.1 through 6.5 below (Hess, 1959; Williamson *et al.*, 1987).

$$\frac{\partial u}{\partial t} = -(u\frac{\partial u}{\partial x} + v\frac{\partial u}{\partial y} + w\frac{\partial u}{\partial z}) - \frac{1}{\rho}\frac{\partial p}{\partial x} + 2\Omega(v\sin\varphi - w\cos\varphi) \qquad \text{Eq. 6.1}$$

$$\frac{\partial v}{\partial t} = -(u\frac{\partial v}{\partial x} + v\frac{\partial v}{\partial y} + w\frac{\partial v}{\partial z}) - \frac{1}{\rho}\frac{\partial p}{\partial y} - 2\Omega u\sin\varphi \qquad \text{Eq. 6.2}$$

$$\frac{\partial w}{\partial t} = -(u\frac{\partial w}{\partial x} + v\frac{\partial v}{\partial y} + w\frac{\partial w}{\partial z}) - \frac{1}{\rho}\frac{\partial p}{\partial z} - 2\Omega u\cos\varphi - g \qquad \text{Eq. 6.3}$$

$$\frac{\partial \rho}{\partial t} = -(u\frac{\partial \rho}{\partial x} + v\frac{\partial \rho}{\partial y} + w\frac{\partial \rho}{\partial z}) - \rho(\frac{\partial u}{\partial x} + \frac{\partial v}{\partial y} + \frac{\partial w}{\partial z}) \qquad \text{Eq. 6.4}$$

$$\frac{\partial p}{\partial t} = -(u\frac{\partial p}{\partial x} + v\frac{\partial p}{\partial y} + w\frac{\partial p}{\partial z}) - \gamma p(\frac{\partial u}{\partial x} + \frac{\partial v}{\partial y} + \frac{\partial w}{\partial z}) \qquad \text{Eq. 6.5}$$

where u, v, and w are the components of motion for a parcel of air in the East (x), North (y), and upward (z) directions, respectively; ρ is the density; and p is the pressure. These five variables can theoretically be solved as a function of time (t) using these five equations if the constants Ω = the Coriolis parameter, g = the acceleration due to gravity, and γ = a gas constant for air are specified. In addition, the initial and boundary conditions must be known. In Eqs. 6.1-6.3 ϕ is the latitude of the parcel. The conservation of water mass and the cloud physics equations for converting water vapor to precipitation must be added to these equations if it is desired to compute cloud formation and precipitation. Typically, these equations are added in a parameterized form after the hydrodynamic fields are solved. Heat interactions due to phase changes are introduced between iterations of the hydrodynamic fields.

Although most climate models use some type of finite differencing technique to solve the differential equations, the Community Climate Model (CCM1) used here, also uses a spectral analysis technique to avoid numerical instabilities near the poles. GCM's are very expensive to operate because they require large amounts of computing time and massive memories.

Description of the Community Climate Model

The Community Climate Model was originally developed from a spectral model produced by W. Bourke, B. McAvaney, K. Puri, and R. Thurling (Williamson *et al.*, 1987). The first version, CCM0A, was quickly updated and called CCM0B. CCM0B offered a new approach to climate studies in that it was less of a forecasting program and more of a simulation program. This means that instead of generating data based on statistical records, the program was more deterministic in producing output. The traditional statistical program was more likely to develop errors as time elapsed. The new model allowed runs to be made for longer lengths of time with less deviation. Since then, improvements from many contributors brought about the version, CCM1. The improvements have addressed major aspects of the program such as horizontal and vertical diffusion, convection, mixing, and radiational absorption (Williamson *et al.*, 1987). Since the 1980's CCM1 has been improved even further with components which account for biological and cryogenic systems. These later versions have been called CCM2, Genesis, etc.

CCM1 operates with several horizontal spectral resolutions. The resolution used by most modelers and the one used in this effort is the R15 option, meaning each grid point is separated by 4.5° latitude and 7.5° longitude resulting in a Gaussian grid of 40 latitude grid points at each of 48 longitudes over the surface of the earth for a total of 1920 grid points. The R15 option specifies that 15 terms are used when converting the grid point data to a spectral equation in the algorithm. CCM1 manages the different atmospheric variables by constructing grid boxes at the grid points and calculating forces and transfer rates for each box. The resolution is fairly crude in handling topographic variations, resulting in considerable smoothing over high relief areas. Precipitation tends to be underestimated on the windward side and overestimated on the leeward side of high relief areas, such as in Alaska and southeast Asia (Shultz *et al.*, 1992). Higher resolution options are available and provide increased precision, but are not as frequently used as the R15 option because of the high amount of computing time required.

Vertically, the sigma-coordinate system (Washington and Parkinson, 1986) is used where σ is defined as:

$$\sigma = \frac{P}{P_s} \qquad \text{Eq. 6.6}$$

where P is the atmospheric pressure at the given point and P_s is the surface pressure vertically below the given point. CCM1 accounts for twelve vertical levels ranging from $\sigma = 0$ at the top level ($P = 0$) and $\sigma = 1$ at the surface ($P = P_s$). A detailed description of the CCM1 is given in Williamson and Williamson (1987).

Paleoclimates and Future Climates

After comparing the model predictions under current conditions, the model can be used to simulate climates which do not exist today. The studies fall into two categories: paleoclimates and future climates. CCM1 has been used extensively for both. Modeling of future climates has been more controversial because there are no physical data with which to make comparisons of the results. One of the most controversial future climate studies has been the simulation of increased carbon dioxide concentration on temperature. Manabe and Stouffer (1980), Moore *et al.* (1992), and Washington and Meehl (1984) have conducted simulations with double, triple, and even quadruple concentrations of carbon dioxide compared to that of today. The indication of a warming of the atmosphere by as much as 5°C for a doubling of carbon dioxide concentration has resulted in the questionable decision to enforce limitations on exhaust emissions in developed countries and clearing of forests in third world countries.

One of the most studied paleoclimates is that of an "Ice Age" era. A number of variables from ice and ocean sediment cores suggest periods of colder climate at varying latitudes. Shackleton *et al.* (1983) have examined carbon dioxide levels and Thompson *et al.* (1995) have examined oxygen isotope ratios in ice cores. Using ocean sediment cores, Fontugne *et al.* (1994) have been able to construct paleoclimates from pollen and faunal measurements. Although the ice and ocean sediment data is in general agreement that the global climate was at one time significantly cooler, there is no evidence pointing to the *cause* of this change in climate. This is where climate models can be of great value.

Uniformly Warm Oceans

An issue that has received a lot of attention in climate modeling is the Cretaceous climate. Paleoclimate data from high latitudes suggest a warm, equable climate during the Cretaceous period, existing 100 million years ago according to conventional dating of the geologic column (Barron and Washington, 1982a). Conventional interpretations can not explain these warm temperatures based on today's climate patterns. This has left climatologists to speculate on how the earth would have to change in order for high latitudes to experience warmer temperatures than those observed today. Vardiman (1986) and Rush (1990) have constructed a water vapor canopy model for the earth. This canopy is thought to have existed before the Genesis Flood, and its collapse would have occurred during the Flood. The canopy would result in warm surface temperatures across the entire globe, thereby explaining fossils of reptiles and tropical plants that have been found at high latitudes (Oard, 1990). If the vapor canopy theory is rejected, another mechanism must be found to justify the warm surface temperatures.

In an effort to explain warm, equable climates Barron and Washington (1982a and 1982b) examined the results of simulations conducted on an NCAR GCM. They attempted to produce warm land-surface temperatures using mid-Cretaceous geography and prescribed sea-surface temperatures. The model was adjusted to use Cretaceous geography, meaning the continents were much closer together than today. The sea-surface temperatures were prescribed to a smaller equator-to-pole gradient than what exists today, resulting in warmer high-latitude and polar sea-surface temperatures. Prior to Barron and Washington's study it was believed that the changes would induce a poleward displacement of major circulation patterns, and an overall "sluggish" circulation of the atmosphere (Barron and Washington, 1982b). It was also believed that the warmer oceans would supply heat to the continental interiors, thereby explaining the tropical paleoclimate data that has been found at high latitudes. From this study it was shown that changes in geography and the equator-to-pole sea-surface temperature gradient cannot explain a warm, equable climate.

The model results showed that the warmer oceans did not warm the continents, instead the continental interiors were cold and a large surface temperature gradient occurred at the ocean-continent boundaries. While some warming did occur at mid-latitudes, the study could not justify the plant and reptile fossils found in areas like Alaska and Antarctica. More importantly, the study showed that the atmosphere did not become "sluggish" when the equator-to-pole gradient was decreased. In fact, the zonally averaged surface wind speeds *increased* over standard conditions (Barron and Washington; 1982a, 1982b). These are the kinds of conditions that would be necessary to produce rapid ice sheet growth and offers support to the Biblical "Ice Age" model presented in this paper.

A Sensitivity Study of Warm Sea-Surface Temperature

A sensitivity study was conducted by Spelman (1996) for four different sea-surface temperature distributions using the NCAR CCM1 model. The model was run in the perpetual mode, which means the solar heating was not varied seasonally like the earth actually experiences but was held at a constant amount and distribution of radiation. The first run was made with boundary conditions prescribed in the NCAR documentation (Williamson and Williamson, 1987; Williamson *et al.*, 1987; and Bath *et al.*, 1991). The duration of the run was 360 days of perpetual January conditions and is referred to as the *standard* run. The second run was made with all other conditions the same as the standard run but with the initial sea-surface temperature set at 0°C for the poles and uniformly warming to 30°C at the equator. The third run had the initial sea-surface temperature set to 15°C at the poles and uniformly increased to 30°C at the equator. The fourth run was made with a uniform sea-surface temperature of 30°C from the poles to the equator. These sea-surface temperatures were prescribed and remained invariant throughout the length of the run. The other variables, such as surface pressure and precipitation, were allowed to change as the model progressed.

Surface pressure over the oceans increased only slightly when sea-surface temperature was held constant. Surface pressure over the continents decreased with an increase in land-surface temperature. Precipitation increased at high latitudes and along ocean-continental boundaries with warmer sea-surface temperature. Large areas of precipitation rates greater than 20 mm per day occurred in polar regions and along continental boundaries. Some areas of precipitation rates greater than 40 mm per day occurred (See Fig. 6.2). The land-to-ocean surface temperature gradient was greatest with the warmest oceans. This gradient created strong winds that moved parallel to continental boundaries. Winds above the surface increased at high latitudes with little variation between the runs. Air temperature and winds high above the surface were only slightly influenced by warmer oceans. Equilibrium was reached quickly by CCM1

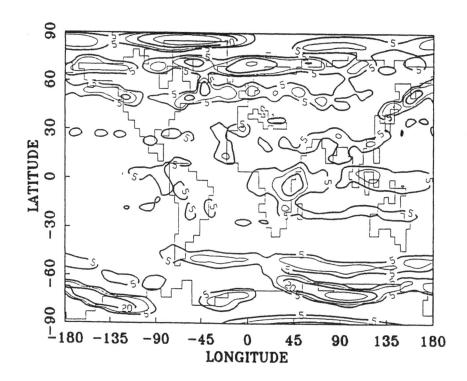

Figure 6.2 Precipitation contours from day 360 of the run with uniform 30°C oceans. Outer dark contour - 5 mm/day, next light contour - 10 mm/day, inner dark contour - 20 mm/day, and inner most light contour - 40 mm/day.

in the perpetual January mode. For all the variables considered, no appreciable changes occurred after the first 90 days of the runs.

Based on the model results found above the following applications to the Flood model can be made. If the oceans remained warm, they would have continued to supply moisture and precipitation to continental and polar regions. In areas where the temperature was consistently below freezing, precipitation would have been in the form of snow. If, after the Genesis Flood, the oceans were warm from equator to pole, as simulated in this study, and well mixed from top to bottom, the warm ocean effect would have continued for many years, allowing ice sheets to form where temperatures remained below freezing. Volcanic aerosols and a high surface albedo created by the growing volume of ice, would have kept the land cold, allowing significant ice sheet growth. A snowfall rate of 20 millimeters per day could produce a 2-kilometer thick ice sheet in under 300 years in the polar regions.

Simulation of Precipitation Induced by Hot Mid-Ocean Ridges

Vardiman (1998) ran the CCM1 model in the standard mode above but with selected patterns of hot sea-surface temperatures to simulate the effect of hot mid-ocean ridges on precipitation and wind fields. Fig. 6.3 shows the surface grid points held at hot ridge temperatures. Runs were made with ridge temperatures of 30°C, 50°C, and 70°C. Fig. 6.4 shows the precipitation rate and Figs. 6.5 and 6.6 the horizontal wind speed at 500 mb for a ridge

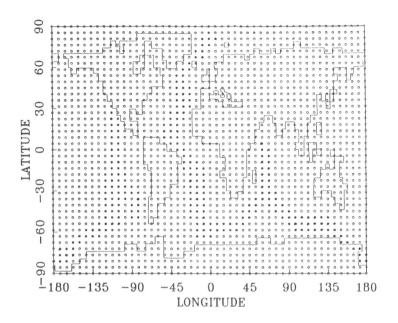

Figure 6.3 Grid points used in CCM1. Darkened circles are grid points over the mid-ocean ridge.

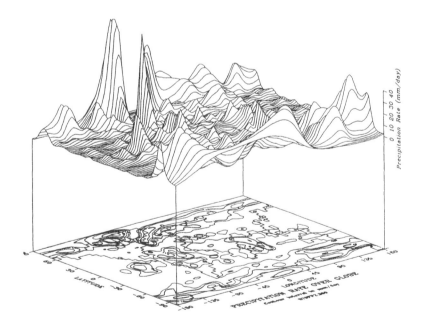

Figure. 6.4 Precipitation rate in mm/day on the globe for grid points over a ridge of 70°C. Contour interval in the lower diagram are shown at 5, 10, 40, and 80 mm/day increments. The upper diagram shows the same precipitation on a 3D surface.

temperature of 70°C over the globe. Increased ridge temperature lead to increased precipitation over and downwind of the ridge, increased horizontal wind speed in the lower atmosphere, decreased horizontal wind speed aloft, and an increase in the frequency of upward vertical velocity over the ridges. The rate of precipitation exceeded 20 mm/day over large portions of the ridge and was up to 80 mm/day in limited areas for a 70°C ridge. It was greatest over Greenland and the North Atlantic south of Greenland. Precipitation also extended downwind over portions of the ocean away from the ridge, toward polar regions, and into continental areas, particularly near the equator. Precipitation rates and areas of coverage increased globally as the ridge temperature was increased.

The horizontal winds from the surface through the troposphere were westerly from mid-latitudes poleward in both hemispheres and easterly at equatorial latitudes. Between 30° - 45° north and south latitudes the winds were relatively calm in what are called the doldrums. The heat and moisture over hot ridges caused the frequency of downward motions to decrease and upward motions to increase. Precipitation in the doldrums fell over the mid-ocean ridge. However, increased precipitation over the mid-ocean ridge in equatorial latitudes drifted westward and precipitation in polar regions drifted eastward to fall on continental regions.

It is apparent that hot mid-ocean ridges cause a large change in the distribution of winds and precipitation globally. The effects are not limited only to locations near the ridge. Average global horizontal winds speed in the lower atmosphere were increased as the ridge temperature was increased. Precipitation rates and coverage increased, particularly toward the polar regions as the ridge temperature was increased. Some of the precipitation patterns seemed to match those which occurred during the "Ice Age."

These effects appear to be consistent with many of the expectations from Scripture and inferred distributions of snow and ice coverage during the "Ice Age." If the Genesis Flood was a global, catastrophic event described in Scripture, it would have been accompanied by large crustal movements, formation of mid-ocean ridges, and significant heating of the ocean in locations near the ridges. This heating would have produced increased evaporation over the oceans and precipitation over the continents and polar regions. The model simulations have shown that the distribution of precipitation in the polar regions are similar to the distribution of snow and ice which occurred during the "Ice Age." This match increases confidence in the catastrophic, tectonic flood model of Wise *et al.* (1994).

CCM1 simulates the global dynamic and hydrological effects caused by a change in sea-surface temperature like those suggested in this paper. However, it can not simulate smaller-scale features and even hotter temperatures which may have been generated during the actual Flood event. The formation of "hypercanes" as suggested by Emanuel (1995) would probably occur under the conditions assumed in this research and could be an additional factor on precipitation and wind.

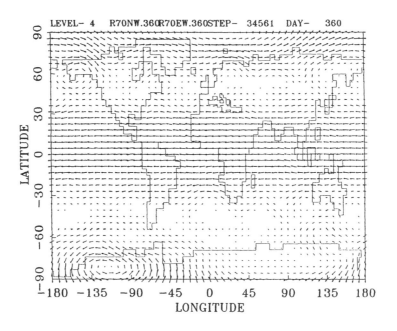

Figure 6.5　Horizontal wind field at a pressure of 110 mb (15 km).

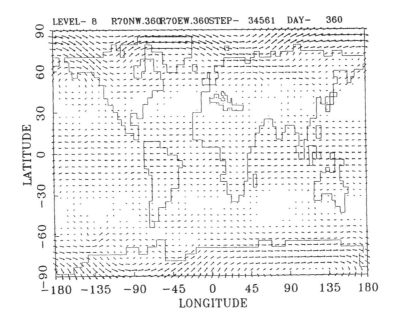

Figure 6.6　Horizontal wind field at a pressure of 500 mb (5 km).

Climate Model Limitations

Climate models are under constant revision in order to improve components such as resolution, heat transport, cloud formation, coupled ocean-atmosphere activity, and precipitation estimates. Even though the models have made great strides in the past two decades, complete confidence cannot be held in their abilities to accurately simulate the climate. The inaccuracies are obvious when attempting to model the current climate because we can compare the results to direct observations. When the models are used to simulate past or future climate scenarios, the limitations affect our confidence in the results. One way that investigators try to verify model results is to compare them to paleoclimate data, such as ice and ocean sediment cores. This method is greatly dependent on the accuracy of the physical data.

Barron and Washington (1982b) have identified three limitations to understanding the climate over geologic time. First, it is not possible to describe past climates completely by paleoclimate data. Second, it is not known for sure how external climate factors like insolation and atmospheric composition might have varied in the past. Third, the climate system at present is not fully understood, therefore hindering our ability to model the system. Due to these limitations, Barron and Washington (1982b) have concluded that we are presently incapable of completely simulating the climate of any geologic period.

Evidence of these limitations can be seen in the lack of agreement among scientists who use climate models. For example, on the subject of the earth's future climate, contrasting viewpoints are found. From Hays *et al*. (1976):

> "A model of future climate based on the observed orbital-climate relationships, but ignoring anthropogenic effects, predicts that the long-term trend over the next several thousand years is toward extensive Northern Hemisphere glaciation."

Conversely, Reid (1991) concludes:

> "As far as the future is concerned, there is no obvious reason to question the predictions of future global warming due to the atmosphere's increasing burden of greenhouse gases. Unless there are serious deficiencies in our understanding, the conclusion that the greenhouse warming will eventually overwhelm other natural effects of climate variability seems inescapable."

Despite the limitations and varying conclusions, climate modeling is still a worthwhile endeavor. Much progress has been made since its beginning and improvements will certainly continue to be made.

CHAPTER 7

FUTURE RESEARCH WITH MM5

Hurricane Modeling

Hurricanes are one of nature's most devastating phenomena. They occur in the warm, moist environment of the near equatorial latitudes where conditions are right for the development of these monster storms. Fig. 7.1 shows an example of a hurricane -- in this case, Gladys in the Gulf of Mexico during 1968. Gladys filled the entire Gulf with spiral rain bands from the coast of Mexico to the Florida peninsula. More dramatic examples of animated hurricanes may be found on the CD in the pocket at the back of this monograph. Hurricanes included on the CD are Mitch, Luis, and Guiermo.

Hurricanes are born in the warm waters of the tropical latitudes (20°N to 20°S). The tropics supply necessary ingredients for hurricane development - wide expanses of warm ocean; air that is both warm and humid; and typically weak upper-level winds in the same direction as the surface winds. When sea-surface temperatures (SSTs) are above 79°F (26°C) in tropical regions, conditions are ripe for hurricane development.

Riehl (1954), Gray (1968), Simpson (1971), and Herbert (1977) have developed criteria to gauge the likelihood of tropical disturbances developing into hurricanes in the northern hemisphere. In summary, the criteria favorable for development include 1) above normal temperatures aloft, 2) a cloud mass north and east of the tropical wave axis, 3) abundant moisture at low levels in the atmosphere, 4) warm sea-surface temperatures, 5) weak upper-level wind shears, 6) surface cyclonic vorticity, and 7) advection of vorticity at upper levels. Wind shear is a change in wind speed or direction with height. Vorticity is a measure of the circular motion of the atmosphere.

During the Genesis Flood and for some time afterward many of these conditions were probably present on the earth. Some of the criteria probably reached extreme degrees, such as elevated sea-surface temperatures. If mid-ocean ridges formed rapidly during and immediately following the Flood, sea-surface temperatures could have easily exceeded 30°C, possibly approaching 100°C in places. These conditions favor the formation of convective cells into large-scale systems and then into intense cyclonic storms. It is recognized that the warmer the sea-surface temperature the more intense the hurricane. Gigantic hurricanes with horizontal winds approaching 600 mph and vertical winds exceeding 100 mph, termed hypercanes, have been modeled by Emanuel et al. (1995) in hopes of providing a mechanism for the mass extinction of dinosaurs. The widespread formation of hypercanes sweeping across bare continents following the Flood would have produced catastrophic rainfall and erosion in lower latitudes and massive snowfall in polar latitudes.

In light of these influencing factors, hurricane formation is of great interest to anyone pondering the meteorological and climate events during and following the Great Flood in the days of Noah. One of the first steps which is intended to be taken at ICR in hurricane modeling is to confirm the intensification of hurricanes as a function of sea-surface temperature, particularly at extreme values. Emanuel (1987) and Holland (1997) have studied this effect but not in the range of 35°C to 50°C which is intended at ICR.

A mesoscale meteorology model (MM5) has been installed on one of the computers at ICR and is being used for this effort. MM5 was developed by The Pennsylvania State University (Anthes and Warner, 1978; Anthes *et al.*, 1987) and is currently being supported by NCAR (Dudhia, 1993). Data for the environment and Hurricane Florence, which occurred in the Gulf of Mexico in 1988, was acquired from NASA Goddard. MM5 was run using these input data for 34 hours and for several higher levels of sea-surface temperature between 30°C and 50°C. The hurricane intensified rapidly at warmer temperatures and reached precipitation rates almost ten times that of the actual hurricane. Horizontal and vertical wind speeds increased dramatically as well. Figs. 7.2 through 7.5 show the increase in cloud-water content and rain-water content of Hurricane Florence simulated by MM5 every 12 hours with a sea-surface temperature of 45°C. Animated displays of this MM5 simulation for water content and horizontal winds at several levels are also included on the CD in the back of this monograph. Nancy Zavacky, a graduate student at ICR, will report the exact values and a complete analysis when she completes her thesis.

The effects of small patches of hot sea-surface temperatures on hurricane development will be explored in future work. This effort will attempt to simulate the patterns likely to have developed over hot mid-ocean ridges as they formed. It is possible that hurricanes may tend to preferentially form and their movements be affected by the patterns of hot surface water. For extremely high temperatures hurricanes may even become stationary over hot spots. At least, elongated patterns of hot surface water could be the source of intense hurricanes which eventually reach land.

Once hurricane formation and intensification is better understood, correlations between the presence of mid-ocean ridges near the continents and erosion may be possible. Of particular interest are regions in southeast Asia and western Africa. Could some of the major erosional features found there be associated with heavy rain from hurricane formation immediately following the Flood. In a similar manner, correlations between the location of heaviest ice sheet development during the "Ice Age" and likely hurricane tracks from the mid-ocean ridges may be possible. Here the major interest would be in understanding why such a thick ice sheet developed across northern North America while so little ice apparently formed in Asia. The relatively narrow band of ice in northern Europe and Scandinavia may hold a clue to this phenomenon.

It has been known for many years that when hurricanes move into cooler water they lose their energy source and decrease in strength. NASA recently reported that some of the new weather satellites are able to "see" down through hurricanes to the ocean surface below. Data from these new satellites show that sea-surface temperatures cool beneath hurricanes by as much as 5 - 10°F by their action. Fig. 7.6 shows a cool "footprint" for hurricane Bonnie as it approached the U.S. coast. Hurricane Danielle following Bonnie later decreased in intensity when it crossed this path of cool water. Hurricanes are viewed by most experts today as gigantic heat engines which extract energy from the ocean surface and transport it into the atmosphere.

Other Mesoscale Modeling

Although hurricane modeling with MM5 is very exciting and potentially valuable, there are several other projects on which MM5 can be used. MM5 is a mesoscale model, which means it is best used for weather features that have dimensions on the order of tens to thousands of kilometers and time scales on the order of hours to days. This is in contrast to the Global Climate Models (GCMs) which are intended to simulate global climate processes which have space scales of tens of thousands of kilometers and time scales of months to years. MM5 has easily changeable space and time steps which can be set for a weather phenomenon as small as a single cloud or to a regional weather event. Normally, MM5 uses a set of grids in which one grid defines the large-scale wind, temperature, and moisture fields and a second grid makes computations at smaller space and time steps nested within the larger grid. Real data from various archived sources like the Weather Bureau or the U.S. Navy may be accessed to establish the larger grid's initial and changing values. Once the larger scale conditions are established, MM5 then simulates an event by solving the primitive meteorological equations on the grid points of a smaller nested grid.

Some of the mesoscale projects slated for future work are: 1) Dispersion of oxygen isotopes in snow over polar regions, 2) Changes in flow patterns and precipitation over the Colorado River Basin due to higher orographic features during the "Ice Age," and 3) Hurricane generated hummocky cross-beddding over shallow water such as on the Florida Peninsula.

Dispersion of Oxygen Isotopes

In chapter 4 of this monograph a model for the dispersion of oxygen isotopes in the polar regions was described. A simple air-flow model was developed and an even simpler set of LaGrangian microphysics was imbedded in the flow fields. Although the computations agreed with the anticipated results, the study did not generate great confidence because of the simplistic techniques used and the prescribed flow fields. It would seem that a more thorough attempt should be made to simulate this situation with a model like MM5. The flow fields in MM5 respond to the specified boundary conditions in accordance with the primitive meteorological equations and the model contains more accurate microphysics. The model could be run for today's conditions which are not growing large ice sheets and for conditions hypothesized to have occurred during the "Ice Age" when ice sheets were growing rapidly. If the trends in oxygen isotopes measured in ice cores from Greenland and Antarctica can be duplicated, more confidence in the recent formation and retreat of polar ice sheets will be achieved.

Changes in Flow Patterns and Precipitation over the Colorado River Basin

Also in chapter 4 of this monograph a calculation was described for the amount and rate of snowfall which likely fell during the "Ice Age" on the mountains of the Colorado River Basin. The amount was sufficient that the mountains in and surrounding the Colorado River Basin would probably have been increased in elevation by several thousand feet during the "Ice Age." It is well known that the height of a mountain barrier creates a strong orographic effect on wind fields and precipitation. Not only are vertical winds and precipitation increased for higher mountains, but horizontal wind flows may be blocked and diverted. MM5 would seem to be a good model to use in studying wind fields and precipitation in the Colorado River Basin during the "Ice Age." Comparisons of conditions during the "Ice Age" and today are likely to be instructive. Higher mountain barriers not only influence local wind fields and precipitation, but also may possibly influence the jet stream and storm tracks. It has already been suggested by Kurtzbach (1987) that the massive ice sheets in northern North America diverted the jet stream southward over North America during the "Ice Age," causing a wetter southwest. Possibly more was at work in this diversion of the jet stream than just the influence of a large, shallow mountain of ice in Canada.

Hurricane-Generated Hummocky Cross-Bedding

Hummocky cross-bedding has been observed in numerous geological formations such as the Chattanooga Shale deposits in central Tennessee and the Rock Springs and Blair Sandstone Formations in southwestern Wyoming. It is a distinctive pattern of generally horizontal, sedimentary strata which are mounded and interleaved at the boundaries. It is believed that these deposits and many others like them may have been formed by hurricanes over shallow seas (Schieber, 1994; Finley, 1992; Srivastava, 1972; and Barron, 1989). If the effects of pressure and wind at the bottom of a hurricane can be translated from the upper surface of a shallow water layer to the movement of sand on the bottom, it may be possible to use MM5 to study the formation of hummocky cross-bedded deposits in places like Florida. Recent digs in sandy layers of Florida have uncovered Mammoths, saber-toothed tigers, and other Pliocene and Pleistocene deposits interleaved with mammals, birds, and plants of the Holocene period. Is it possible that post-Flood hurricanes buried plants and animals of many different species in the same location and time? Comparison of patterns of hurricane-generated strata with observed strata today in Florida may help tie catastrophic Flood processes with geology of the past.

Figure 7.1 Hurricane Gladys in the Gulf of Mexico in 1968 (NASA).

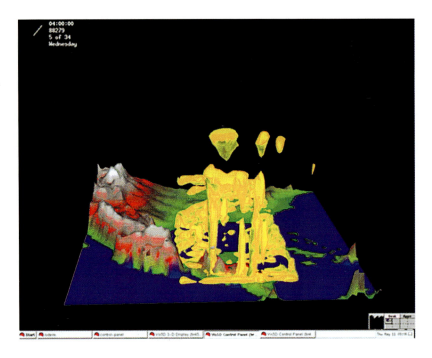

Figure 7.2   Simulation of Hurricane Florence in the Gulf of Mexico at 5 hours after a large rectangular area of sea surface is heated to 45°C (Yellow is cloud water, green is Rain).

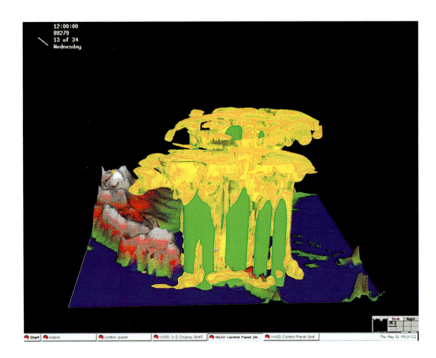

Figure 7.3   Simulation of Hurricane Florence in the Gulf of Mexico at 13 hours after a large rectangular area of sea surface is warmed to 45°C (Yellow is cloud water, green is rain).

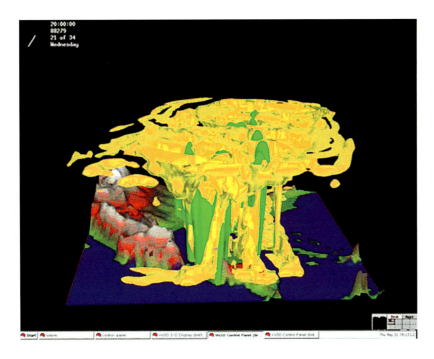

Figure 7.4 Simulation of Hurricane Florence in the Gulf of Mexico at 21 hours after a large rectangular area of sea surface is warmed to 45°C (Yellow is cloud water, green is rain).

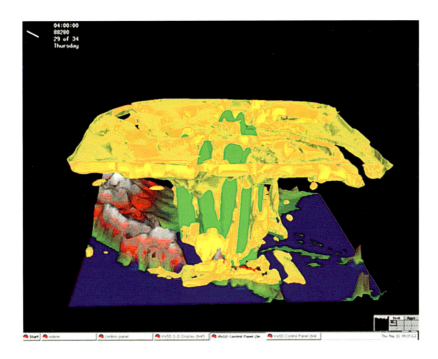

Figure 7.5 Simulation of Hurricane Florence in the Gulf of Mexico at 29 hours after a large rectangular area of sea surface is warmed to 45°C (Yellow is cloud water, green is rain).

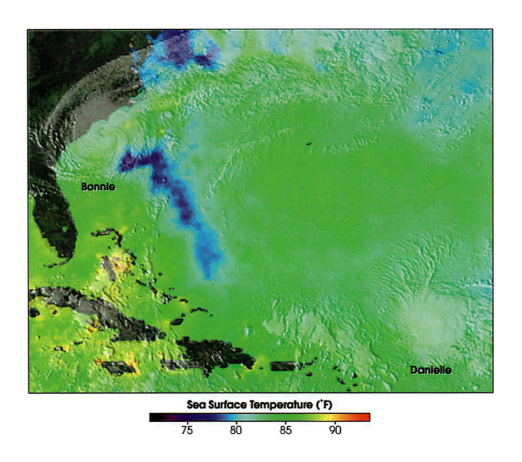

Figure 7.6   A cold "footprint" produced by Hurricane Bonnie off the East Coast of the U. S. in 1998 (NASA). Bonnie may be seen as the ghostly feature centered on the coast of Georgia and South Carolina. The cold footprint shows as a blue feature extending southeastward from Bonnie into the Atlantic where it had just traversed. Danielle may be seen in the lower right-hand corner of the picture moving west-northwest toward the footprint.

CHAPTER 8

COMPUTER HARDWARE AND SOFTWARE USED AT ICR

ICR effectively began paleoclimate modeling in the summer of 1983 when I started work on the escape of helium from the earth's atmosphere. However, I had been doing research on a vapor canopy model even before associating with ICR. These early studies were done with purchased time on a CDC 7600 mainframe computer at the U.S. Bureau of Reclamation Engineering and Research Center in Denver, Colorado, a small Apple II computer at Christian Heritage College, and my personal Turbo XT IBM-compatible PC. I used FORTRAN II, FORTRAN IV and FORTRAN 77 languages for various model calculations on these machines.

In 1988 an IBM-compatible 386 with a math co-processor was purchased by ICR for the Astrogeophysics Department and was the main workhorse for over five years. It had three versions of FORTRAN installed at various times, but the most convenient version was a menu-driven form of FORTRAN 77 distributed by McFarland, Inc. A plotting library called Plot88 was purchased to allow graphical displays to be generated within the FORTRAN program. A black and white laser printer was donated by Steve Low and his associates at Hewlett-Packard which upgraded the quality of the graphical output dramatically. Several other application programs were also purchased for this computer such as the Biomedical Data Package (BMDP) for PCs, a statistical package which allowed handy statistical and graphical manipulation of large quantities of data. BMDP is a version of a mainframe statistical package used by the author and many other researchers for over 25 years.

The major limitation on the 386 was its speed. When David Rush was conducting runs of LOWTRAN 7 modified to simulate the vertical heating in his vapor canopy model, it took about six weeks to complete a single run, operating day and night. Because of the possibility that a power outage would disrupt a run, David designed his code to be restartable. This way, if a run was disrupted, he could restart part way through without having to recompute everything from the beginning. David ran over ten of these 6-week projects before he completed his thesis.

Before we could use the code for CCM1, ICR needed to upgrade its computing power. In 1992 Steve Low and his associates donated two Hewlett-Packard 486s which were five times as fast as the old 386. One of these machines was used at ICR and the other sent to Herman Daily for his use in programming and debugging the CCM1 model and later programs for ICR. A few years later Steve Low donated a Hewlett-Packard 586 which was about three times faster than the 486. All of these machines used DOS and Windows 3.1 or 95 as the primary operating systems. However, in order to take advantage of a new Digital FORTRAN compiler which had the ability of 32-bit precision, the OS-2 operating system was installed on the 586 and double precision programmed into the FORTRAN code to effectively achieve 64-bit precision, similar to a mainframe computer. This was done to check out some problems which arose from some of Karen Spelman's computations on CCM1.

Finally, in late 1998, a high-end Pentium II, IBM-compatible, 400 Mhz machine was purchased to run MM5 and associated programs. The Linux operating system was used on this machine which allowed the original mainframe code which operated unto UNIX to now be operated under a Portland Group version of FORTRAN 77. A graphical package called VIS5D is operated under Linux and displays the output on a large, high-resolution monitor. This system allows images and movies of 3-dimensional perspective views of storms to be shown and studied. Vertical and horizontal cross sections of several sets of data like temperature, wind, and cloud moisture may be displayed. Nancy Zavacky is using this tool extensively in her thesis on hurricane modeling.

Archival of data and computational results are done in the lab by storage with floppy disks, tapes, Zip disks, and Jaz disks. Writeable CDs have not been purchased yet, but will likely be used in the near future. For large files, there are some incompatibility problems between machines because they do not all have the same storage equipment. So far, this has not been a major problem because most research for a specific project has been confined to a single machine. Only in cases where it is desired to speed up an old program will this likely become a problem.

Because of the need to access email and the Internet to download data, the Astrogeophysics lab has had its own phone line with outside access for several years. Since ICR now has full access to the Internet via its network on a T-1 line throughout the Institute, this system is archaic and may eventually be disconnected. However, in 2000 the Astrogeophysics Department still has slow, outside access.

All five machines purchased by ICR or donated to the Astrogeophysics Department are still operating. The philosophy has been to maintain old machines with original hardware and software and not upgrade them. If a faster machine or a new operating system and software are needed, this is accomplished on a new machine. Consequently, much of the original capability is retained on the machines, old research projects can be resurrected at any time, and new runs made. In addition, this allows multiple students to function in the laboratory simultaneously.

It has been a blessing to watch how the Lord has provided computer equipment and software at just the right time to allow the research to proceed. In fact, the Astrogeophysics Department at ICR has more powerful computer systems available now than I ever had when working for the U.S. Air Force, Colorado State University, or the U.S. Bureau of Reclamation in the past. Fortunately, the correct choices were made to invest in IBM-compatible machines and software over the years. Even major government laboratories like Los Alamos National Laboratories and the National Center for Atmospheric Research are now using machines similar to ours. We have invested little and gotten much back on our expenditures. In addition, we have had many donors who have given money and equipment at the right time. We have also had access to free and discounted software which would have cost hundreds of thousands of dollars if we were to purchase it. Finally, Herman Daily has donated an incredible amount of programming to ICR over the past seven years. What a blessing!

REFERENCES

Aamondt, R.E. and K.M. Case, 1962. Density in a simple model of the exosphere, **Physics of Fluids 5:**1019-1021.

Alley, R.B., Shuman, C.A., Meese, D.A., Gow, A.J., Taylor, K.C., Ram, M., Waddington, E.D., and Mayewski, P.A., 1992. An old, long, abrupt Younger Dryas event in the GISP2 ice core. *In*: **Proceedings of the 1992 Fall Meeting of the American Geophysical Union**, San Francisco, California.

Alley, R.B., Meese, D.A., Shuman, C.A., Gow, A.J., Taylor, K.C., Grootes, P.M., White, J.W.C., Ram, M., Waddington, E.D., Mayewski, P.A., and Zielinski, G.A., 1993. Abrupt increase in Greenland snow accumulation at the end of the Younger Dryas Event. **Nature, 362**:527-529.

Anthes, R.A and T.T. Warner, 1978. Development of hydrodynamic models suitable for air pollution and other mesometeorological studies. **Monthly Weather Review 106**:1045-1078.

Anthes, R.A., E.Y. Hsie and Y.H. Kuo, 1987. Description of the Penn State/NCAR Mesoscale Model Version 4 (MM4). **NCAR/TN-282+STR**, 66pp.

Axford, W.I., 1968. The polar wind and the terrestrial helium budget, **J. of Geophys. Res., Space Physics 73**:6855-6859.

Banks, H.P. and T.E. Holzer, 1969. High-latitude plasma transport: The polar wind, **J. Geophys. Res. 74:**6317-6323.

Barron, E.J., 1989. Severe storms during earth history. **Geological Society of America Bulletin 101:**601-612.

Barron, E.J. and W.M. Washington, 1982a. Cretaceous climate: a comparison of atmospheric simulations with the geologic record. **Palaeogeography, Palaeoclimatology, Palaeoecology 93:**113.

Barron, E.J. and W.M. Washington, 1982b. Atmospheric circulation during warm geologic periods, **Geology 10:**633-636.

Bath, L.M., M.A. Dias, D.L. Williamson, G.S. Williamson, and R.J. Wolski, 1991. **User's Guide to NCAR CCM1**, NCAR Technical Note. (NCAR/TN-286+IA).

Bowen, R., 1991. **Isotopes and Climate**, Elsevier Applied Science, London, 483 pp.

Brandt, J.C. and J.W. Chamberlain, 1960. Density of a neutral gas in a planetary exosphere, **Physics of Fluids 3**:485-486.

Chamberlain, J.W. and D.M. Hunten, 1987. **Theory of Planetary Atmospheres**, 2nd Ed., Academic Press, 481 pp.

Clarke, W.B., M.A. Beg, and H. Craig, 1969. Excess ^{3}He in the sea: Evidence for terrestrial primordial helium, **Earth and Planetary Science Letters, 6:**213-220.

CLIMAP, 1976. The surface of the ice-age earth. **Science, 191**:1131-1144.

CLIMAP, 1981. Seasonal reconstructions of the earth's surface at the last glacial maximum. **Geological Society of America**, map and Chart Series No. 36.

Cloutier, P.A., M.B. McElroy, and F.C. Michel, 1969. Modification of the Martian inonosphere by the solar wind, **J. Geophys. Res. 74**:6215-6227.

Cook, M.A., 1957. Where is the Earth's radiogenic helium? **Nature, 179**:213.

Craig, H., 1961. Isotope variations in meteoritic waters. **Science, 133**:1702-1703.

Craig, H., 1965. The measurement of oxygen isotope paleotemperatures. *In*: **Proceedings of the Spoleto Conference on Stable Isotopes in Oceanographic Studies of Paleotemperatures, 3**:1-24.

Craig, H., W.B. Clarke, and M.A. Beg, 1975. Excess ^{3}He in deep water on the East Pacific Rise, **Earth and Planetary Science Letters 26:**125-132.

Craig, H. and D. Lal, 1961. The production rate of natural tritium, **Tellus 13:** 85-91.

Craig, H. and J.E. Lupton, 1976. Primordial neon, helium, and hydrogen in oceanic basalts, **Earth and Planetary Science Letters 31:**369-385.

Dansgaard, W., 1964. Stable isotopes in precipitation. **Tellus, 16**:436-468.

Dansgaard, W., Johnsen, S.J., Clausen, H.B., and Langway, C.C., Jr., 1971. Climatic record revealed by the Camp Century ice core. *In*: **Late Cenozoic Glacial Ages**, K.K. Turrekian (ed.), Yale Unversity Press, New Haven and London, pp. 37-56.

Dillow, J. C., 1981. **The Waters Above: Earth's Pre-Flood Vapor Canopy**. Moody Press, Chicago, 479 pp.

Dudhia, J., 1993. A nonhydrostatic version of the Penn State-NCAR mesoscale model: Validation tests and simulation of an Atlantic cyclone and cold front. **Monthly Weather Review 121**:1493-1513.

Emanuel, K.A., 1987. The dependence of hurricane intensity on climate. **Nature 326:**483-485.

Emanuel, K.A., K. Speer, R. Rotunno, R. Srivastava, and M. Molina, 1995. Hypercanes: A possible link in global extinction scenarios, **J. of Geophys. Res., 100 D7:**13,755-13,765.

Fahr, H.J. and B. Shizgal, 1983. Modern exospheric theories and their observational relevance, **Rev. of Geophys. and Space Physics 21**:75-124.

Finley, A.K., 1992. **A Study of the Architecture, Heterogeneity, and Interrelationships of the Storm-Wave-Dominated Delta Front and Pro-Delta Facies of the Rock Springs and Blair Formations, Rock Springs, Wyoming**, Thesis (Masters), University of Wyoming, Laramie, Wyoming.

Fontugne, M., M. Arnold, L. Labeyrie, M. Paterne, S.E. Calvert, and J. Duplessy, 1994. Paleoenvironment, sapropel chronology and Nile River discharge during the last 20,000 years as indicated by deep-sea sediment records in the eastern Mediterranean, **Radiocarbon 1994:**75-78.

Gray, W.M., 1968. Global view of the origin of tropical disturbances and storms. **Monthly Weather Review, 96**:669-700

Hays, J.D., Imbrie, J. and Shackleton, J.J., 1976. Variations in the Earth's orbit: pacement of the Ice Ages. **Science, 194**:1121-1132.

Herbert, P.J., 1977. Intensification criteria for tropical depressions in the western North Atlantic. **NOAA Tech. Memo.** SR-83, 25 pp.

Herring, J. and L. Kyle, 1961. Density in a planetary exosphere, **J. Geophys. Res. 66**:1980-1982.

Hess, S.L., 1959. **Introduction to Theoretical Meteorology**, Holt, Rhinehart, and Winston, New York, 362 pp.

Holland, G.J., 1997. The maximum potential intensity of tropical cyclones. **Journal of the Atmospheric Sciences 54**:2519-2541.

Hunten, D.M., 1973. The escape of light gases from planetary atmospheres, **Journal of the Atmospheric Sciences 30:**1481-1494.

Jacobs, G.A., Hurlburt, H.E., Kindle, J.C., Metzger, E.J., Mitchell, J.L., Teague, W.J., and Wallcraft, A.J., 1994. Decade-scale trans-Pacific propagation and warming effects of an El Niño anomaly. **Nature,** 370: 360-363.

Jeans, J.H., 1916. **The Dynamical Theory of Gases**, Cambridge U. Press, 4th Ed. (1925).

Johnsen, S.J., Dansgaard, W., and White, J.W.C., 1989. The Origin of Arctic Precipitation Under Present and Glacial Conditions. **Tellus**, 41B, pp. 452-468.

Jouzel, J., Merlivat, L., and Lorius, C., 1982. Deuterium excess in an East Antarctic ice core suggests higher relative humidity at the oceanic surface during the last glacial maximum. **Nature, 299**:688-691.

Jouzel, J. and Merlivat, L, 1984. Deuterium and oxygen 18 in precipitation: Modeling of the isotopic effect during during snow formation. **Journal of Geophysical Research, 89**:11749-11757.

Jouzel, J. Russel, G.L., Suozzo, R.J., Koster, R.O., White, J.W.C., and Broecker, W.S., 1987. Simulations of HDD and $H_2^{18}O$ atmospheric cycle using the NASA GISS general circulation model: the seasonal cycle for present day conditions. **Journal of Geophysical Research, 92**:14739-14760.

Kennett, J.P., Houtz, R.E., Andrews, P.B., Edwards, A.R., Gostin, V.A., Hajos, M., Hampton, M., Jenkins, D.G., Margolis, S.V., Ovenshine, A.T., and Perch-Nielson, K., 1977. Descriptions of Procedures and Data for Sites 277, 279, and 281 by the Shipboard Party. *In*: **Initial Reports of the Deep Sea Drilling Project, 29**:45-58, 191-202, and 271-285. GPO: Washington, D.C.

Kurtzbach, J.E., 1987. Model simulations of the climatic patterns during the deglaciation of North America. *In*, **North America and Adjacent Oceans during the Last Deglaciation**, *ed.*, W.F. Ruddiman and H.E. Wright, Jr., Geological Society of America, Boulder, CO.

Lennard-Jones, E., 1923. Free paths in a non-uniform rarefied gas with an application to the escape of molecules from an isothermal atmosphere, **Trans. Cambridge Phil. Soc. 22**:523-556.

Lorentz, E.N., 1967. **The Nature and Theory of the General Circulation of the Atmosphere.** WMO Monograph, 161 pp.

Lupton, J.E. and H. Craig, 1975. Excess ^3He in oceanic basalts: Evidence for terrestrial primordial helium, **Earth and Planetary Science Letters 26:**133-139.

MacDonald, G.J.F., 1964. The escape of helium from the earth's atmosphere, *in* **The Origin and Evolution of Atmospheres and Oceans**, P.J. Brancazio and A.G.W. Cameron, eds, John Wiley and Sons, pp. 127-182.

Manabe, S. and R. Stouffer, 1980. Sensitivity of a global climate model to an increase of CO_2 concentration in the atmosphere. **J. of Geophys. Res. 85(C10):**5529-5554.

Mason, B.J., 1971. **The Physics of Clouds**, Second edition, Clarendon Press, Oxford, 671 pp.

Michel, F.C., 1971. Solar wind interaction with planetary atmospheres, **Rev. Geophys** 8:427-440.

Milankovitch, M., 1930: Mathematische Klimalehre und astronomische Theorie der Klimaschwankungen. *In*: **Handbuch der Klimatologie**, I.W. Koppen and R. Geiger (eds.), Gebrudr Borntraeger, Berlin.

Milankovitch, M., 1941. Canon of insolation and the ice age problem (in Yugoslavian), **Serb. Acad. Beorg.**, Spec. Publ. 132. English translation by Israel Program for Scientific Translations, Jerusalem, 1969.

Moore, G.T., D.N. Hayashida, C.A. Ross, and S.R. Jacobson, 1992. Paleoclimate of the Kimmeridgian/Tithonian (late Jurassic) world: I. Results using a general circulation model, **Palaeogeography, Palaeoclimatology, Palaeoecology 93**:113.

Nye, J.F., 1951. The flow of glaciers and ice sheets as a problem in plasticity. **Proc. Roy. Soc. (London), Ser A, 207:**554.

Nye, J.F., 1957. The distribution of stress and velocity in glaciers and ice sheets. **Proc. Roy. Soc. (London), Ser A, 239:**113.

Nye, J.F., 1959. The motion of ice sheets and glaciers. **J. of Glaciology 3**:493.

Oard, M.J., 1986. An ice age within the Biblical time frame. **Proceedings of the First International Conference on Creationism**, *Ed.* by R.E. Walsh, C.L. Brooks, and R.S. Crowell, Vol. II, Technical Symposium Sessions and Additional Topics, Creation Science Fellowship, Pittsburgh, PA, pp. 157-166.

Oard, M.J., 1990. **An Ice Age Caused by the Genesis Flood**. ICR Monograph, Insititute for Creation Research, Santee, CA., 243 pp.

Opik, E.J. and S.F. Singer, 1959. Distribution of density in a planetary exosphere, **Physics of Fluids** 2:653-655.

Opik, E.J., 1960. Distribution of density in a planetary exosphere, **Physics of Fluids** 3:486-488.

Petit, J.R., White, J.W.C., Young, N.W., Jouzel, J., and Korotkevich, Y.S., 1991. Deuterium excess in recent Antarctic snow. **Journal of Geophysical Research, 96**:5113-5122.

Reid, G.C., 1991. Solar total irradiance variations and the global sea surface temperature record. **J. Geophys. Res. 96(D2):**2835.

Rison, W. and H. Craig, 1983: Helium isotopes and mantle volatiles in Loihi Seamount and Hawaiian Island basalts and xenoliths, **Earth and Planetary Science Letters 66**:407-426.

Riehl, H., 1954. **Tropical Meteorology**. New York, McGraw-Hill Book Co.

Rush, D., 1990. **Radiative Equilibrium Temperature Profiles Under a Vapor Canopy**. M.S. Thesis, ICR Graduate School, Santee, CA, 131 pp.

Rush, D. and L. Vardiman, 1990. Pre-Flood Vapor Canopy Radiative Temperature Profiles. **Proceedings of the Second International Conference on Creationism**, Vol. II, Robert E. Walsh and Christopher L. Brooks, Eds., pp. 231-246.

Ryan, B.F., Wishart, E.R., and Shaw, D.E., 1976. The growth rates and densities of ice crystals between -3°C and -21°C. **Journal of the Atmospheric Sciences, 33**:842-850.

Schieber, J., 1994. Evidence for high-energy events and shallow-water deposition in the Chattanooga Shale, Devonian, central Tennessee, USA. **Sedimentary Geology 93**:193-208.

Scrivastava, P., C.W. Stearn, and E.W. Mountjoy, 1972. A Devonian megabreccia at the margin of the Ancient Wall carbonate complex, Alberta. **Bulletin of the Canadian Petroleum Geology 20**:412-438.

Shackleton, N.J. and Kennett, J.P., 1975. Paleotemperture history of the Cenozoic and the initiation of Antarctic glaciation: Oxygen and carbon isotope analyses in DSDP sites 277, 279, and 281. *In*: **Initial Reports of the Deep Sea Drilling Project, 29**:743-755. GPO: Washington, D.C.

Shackleton, N.J., M.A. Hall, J. Line, and C. Shuxi, 1983. Carbon isotope data in core V19-30 confirm reduced carbon dioxide concentration in the ice age atmosphere. **Nature 306**:319.

Shultz, P., E.J. Barron, and J.L. Sloan II, 1992. Assessment of NCAR general circulation model precipitation in comparison with observations. **Palaeography, Palaeoclimatology, Palaeoecology 97**:269.

Simpson, R.H., 1971. The decision process in hurricane forecasting. **NOAA Tech. Memo.**, NWS SR-53.

Spelman, K.E., 1996. **A Sensitivity Study of the Post-Flood Climate Using the NCAR CCM1 Model with a Warm Sea-Surface Temperature**, ICR Thesis, ICR Graduate School, El Cajon, CA, 155 pp.

Spitzer, L., 1949. The terrestrial atmosphere about 300 km., *in* **The Atmospheres of the Earth and Planets**, G.P. Kuiper, ed., Univ. of Chicago Press, pp. 211-247.

Thompson. L.G., E. Mosley-Thompson, M.E. Davis, P.N. Lin, K.A. Henderson, J. Cole-Dai, J.F. Bolzan, and K.B. Liu, 1995. Late glacial stage and Holocene tropical ice core records from Huascaran, Peru. **Science 269:**46.

Vardiman, L., 1986. The Sky Has Fallen, *In*: **Proceedings of the First International Conference on Creationism**, Basic and Educational Sessions, Vol. I, Creation Science Fellowship, Pittsburgh, PA.

Vardiman, L., 1990: **The Age of the Earth's Atmosphere: A Study of the Helium Flux through the Atmosphere**, ICR Monograph, San Diego, CA, 32 pp.

Vardiman, L., 1993. **Ice Cores and the Age of the Earth,** ICR Monograph, San Diego, California, 86pp.

Vardiman, L., 1994. An Analytic Young-Earth Flow Model of Ice Sheet Formation During the "Ice Age", *In*: **Proceedings of the Third International Conference on Creationism**, Robert Walsh, Ed., Creation Science Fellowship, Pittsburgh, PA.

Vardiman, L., 1996. **Sea-Floor Sediment and the Age of the Earth**, ICR Monograph, San Diego, California, 94pp.

Vardiman, L., 1997. Rapid changes in oxygen isotope content of ice cores caused by fractionation and trajectory dispersion near the edge of an ice shelf. **CEN Tech. J. 11:** 52-60.

Vardiman, L., 1998. Numerical simulation of precipitation induced by hot mid-ocean ridges, *In*: **Proceedings of the Fourth International Conference on Creationism**, Robert E. Walsh, *Ed.*, Creation Science Fellowship, Pittsburgh, PA.

Vardiman, L., 2000. Precipitation and runoff in the Colorado River Basin after the Flood, **Creation Research Society Quarterly**, [in press].

Vardiman, L. and K. Bousselot, 1998. Sensitivity Studies on Vapor Canopy Temperature Profiles. **Proceedings of the Fourth International Conference on Creationism**, Robert E. Walsh, Ed., pp. 607-618.

Walker, J.C.G., 1977. **Evolution of the Atmosphere**, Macmillan, 318 pp.

Washington, W.M. and G.A. Meehl, 1984. Seasonal cycle experiment on the climate sensitivity due to a doubling of CO_2 with an atmospheric general circulation model coupled to a simple mixed-layer ocean model. **J. Geophys. Res. 89(D6):**9475.

Washington, W.M. and C.L. Parkinson, 1986. **An Introduction to Three-Dimensional Climate Modeling**, University Science Books, Mill Valley, CA, 422pp.

Wasserburg, J., 1963. Comments on the outgassing of the Earth, *in* **The Origin and Evolution of Atmospheres and Oceans,** P.J. Brancazio and A.G.W. Cameron, eds., John Wiley and Sons, pp 83-84.

Welhan, J.A. and H. Craig, 1983. Methane, hydrogen, and helium in hydrothermal fluids at 21° N on the East Pacific Rise, *in* **Hydrothermal Processes at Seafloor Spreading Centers,** P.A. Rona, K. Bostron, L. Laubier, and K.L. Smith, eds, Plenum, New York, pp 391-440.

Williamson, D.L., J.T. Kiehl, V. Ramanathan, R.E. Dickinson, and J.J. Hack, 1987. Description of the NCAR Community Climate Model (CCM1). **NCAR Technical Note** (NCAR/TN-285+STR).

Williamson, G.S. and D.L Williamson, 1987. Circulation statistics from seasonal and perpetual January and July simulations with the NCAR Community Climate Model (CCM1):R15. **NCAR Technical Note** (NCAR/TN-302+STR).

Wise, K.P., S.A. Austin, J.R. Baumgardner, D.R. Humphreys, A.A. Snelling, and L. Vardiman, 1994. Catastrophic Plate Tectonics: A Global Flood Model of Earth History. **Proceedings of the Third International Conference on Creationism,** Robert E. Walsh, Ed., Creation Science Fellowship, Pittsburgh, PA, pp. 606-621.

Images and animations on CD

Six image files, eight hurricane movies, and three animated model simulations have been stored on the CD on the back cover of this monograph. These files may be read by any IBM compatible computer with a CD drive, sufficient memory, and the appropriate software. The image files are written as *.gif files and *.jpg files. They may be read and displayed by any good graphics software such as Microsoft Paint. The *.eps file requires Adobe Illustrator or Corel Draw to read and display. The movies are written as *.qt files and can be read and displayed with Microsoft Media Player and Apple Quicktime. This software can be downloaded at www.microsoft.com/windows/windowsmedia/en/download/default.asp and www.apple.com/quicktime/ over the Internet. If you already have Microsoft Media Player installed on your machine and have an Internet connection your machine will automatically download Apple Quicktime when you open one of these files. The three animated model simulations are written as *.ppt and must be read and displayed by Microsoft Power Point. These files may be opened directly and displayed if you have Microsoft Power Point installed on your computer. When these files are opened in Power Point, click on <Slide Show> and then <View Show>. If you don't have Power Point installed, you may open the equivalent folders and click on Pngsetup.exe and the same animated model simulations will be shown.

File	Type	Year	Size	Description
Gladys.eps*	Image	1968	42M	Hurricane in Gulf of Mexico
Bonnie.jpg*	Image	1998	70K	Hurricane on coast of South Carolina
P5.gif	Image	1988	166K	Simulation of Hurricane Florence at 5 hours
P13.gif	Image	1988	194K	Simulation of Hurricane Florence at 13 hours
P21.gif	Image	1988	228K	Simulation of Hurricane Florence at 21 hours
P29.gif	Image	1988	233K	Simulation of Hurricane Florence at 29 hours
Luis.qt*	Movie	1995	7.3M	Movie of Hurricane Luis
Luiszoom.qt*	Movie	1995	4.9M	Movie of Hurricane while zooming in to center
Guillermo.qt*	Movie	1997	3.2M	Movie of Hurricane Guillermo with morphing
Mitch.qt*	Movie	1998	0.6M	Movie of Hurricane Mitch
Dennis1.qt*	Movie	1999	1.7M	Movie of Hurricane Dennis, segment 1
Dennis2.qt*	Movie	1999	1.7M	Movie of Hurricane Dennis, segment 2
Dennis3.qt*	Movie	1999	1.6M	Movie of Hurricane Dennis, segment 3
Dennis4.qt*	Movie	1999	1.5M	Movie of Hurricane Dennis, segment 4
FlorenceP.ppt	Animation	1988	6.5M	Animation of Hurricane Florence in perspective**
FlorenceT.ppt	Animation	1988	3.8M	Animation of Hurricane Florence from the top**
FlorenceW.ppt	Animation	1988	5.8M	Animation of Hurricane Florence winds***

* Images and movies denoted with an asterisk are displayed by NASA on the Internet at http://rsd.gsfc.NASA.gov/goes.

** Simulations are shown for 1-hour intervals after the sea-surface temperature was artificially increased to 45°C over a rectangular area 30° wide over the Gulf of Mexico. Yellow is cloud water and green is rain water.

*** Arrows show the speed and direction of the horizontal wind at 5,000 feet above sea level. The length of the arrows is proportional to the speed of the wind.